VOLATILE STATES

VOLATILE STATES

Institutions, Policy, and the Performance
of American State Economies

W. Mark Crain

THE UNIVERSITY OF MICHIGAN PRESS
Ann Arbor

2006   2005   2004   2003   4   3   2   1

A CIP catalog record for this book is available from the British Library.

Library of Congress Cataloging-in-Publication Data

Crain, W. Mark.
    Volatile states : institutions, policy, and the performance of American
state economies / W. Mark Crain.
        p.   cm.
    Includes bibliographical references and index.
    ISBN 0-472-11303-8 (Cloth : alk. paper)
    1. Finance, Public—United States—States.   2. Taxation—United
States—States.   3. U.S. states—Economic policy.   I. Title.

HJ275 .C69   2003
330.973'092—dc21   2002011938

To Nicole

Acknowledgments

I wish to thank several colleagues and friends for taking an interest in this project and for helping me along the way. Richard Boyland, Bryan Caplan, Nicole Crain, Matt Dobra, John Dunham, Jim Miller, Clair Smith, Dean Stansel, Bob Tollison, and Wayne Winegarden offered constructive comments on the manuscript. In addition, four anonymous reviewers for the University of Michigan Press offered detailed suggestions on an earlier draft. Carol Robert assisted cheerfully in the chores required to move the project forward from its crudest stages to the final product. I am grateful to my editor, Ellen McCarthy, for her oversight, encouragement, excitement, and patience. Mary Meade, Kevin Rennells, and Ann Schultz at the University of Michigan Press guided me through the production hoops. Jean Crain and John Gilchrist provided the family push that never allowed me to give up. Alexander Crain and Juliet Crain made me want to connect to at least two readers 20 years down the road. I am also grateful to many students at George Mason University who listened patiently to a host of half-baked ideas. Partial financial support for the project was generously provided by the James M. Buchanan Center for Political Economy, the Center for Study of Public Choice, the Mercatus Center, and the Phillip Morris Management Corporation. All errors remain my responsibility.

Contents

Illustrations

Tables

Economic and Fiscal Performance in a Mean-Variance Perspective

American states ended the twentieth century on a winning streak. Most had participated in an uninterrupted eight-year economic expansion that lifted living standards to record levels and reduced unemployment rates to thirty-five-year lows. This string of favorable economic events, coupled with a progressive tax structure, caused a surge in state government coffers. State legislators and governors wrestled over what to do with this flood of new revenues, relishing the choice between cutting taxes and expanding their favorite projects. The forces favoring new spending basically won that contest. The typical state budget in the 1990s outpaced state income growth by nearly 1 percentage point annually. At the same time, federal government spending declined as a share of national income, effectively shifting power from Washington to the states.

Those were heady days in the state capitals. Thousands of state politicians had never shared responsibility for a revenue shortfall. Fewer than half of elected state lawmakers had held office long enough to experience hard fiscal times.

The economic winning streak ended early in the new millennium, and the fiscal tide began to turn. In 2001 many state economies began to sputter even before the terrorists attacked the World Trade Center and the Pentagon and new risks to homeland security became a reality. In that year, 44 states reported revenue collections that were below expectations, requiring unpleasant choices not confronted for a decade: spending cuts, tax increases, increasing debt, and dips into rainy-day funds.

Looking back at the 1970–99 period, one finds recurring episodes of major economic stress that squeezed state revenues: 1990–91, 1982, and 1975. Even in these earlier periods of national recession, we discover vast differences in how the individual states fared, how each reacted to changing economic circumstances, and how their economies and budgets bounded and rebounded. As a general matter, few states mirror the "national" economy. Yet the notion of a "U.S. economy" routinely dominates the way we encapsulate, aggregate, and characterize economic conditions that are actually quite unalike at the state level.

In the final three decades of the twentieth century, living standards in the United States increased by 50 percent, or by about $11,500 per person (in 2000 dollars). In North Carolina, the state growth champion, real income rose by nearly $13,000 per person, a 64 percent rise. In Alaska, the state laggard, income grew by 28 percent, less than half the rate in North Carolina. Of course, one might write off Alaska's poor showing to the vicissitudes of oil prices. But what about California's relatively anemic 37 percent growth or Ohio's below-average 42 percent growth? Economic performance in these and other states paled in comparison to the 60 percent plus real growth in states such as Colorado, Massachusetts, and Virginia.

Why do the American state economies grow at such vastly different rates and manifest wide differences in living standards? This question rightfully occupies a prominent place in the history of economic analysis. Few issues in social science are more worthwhile than the sources of rising living standards. This study joins the discourse by examining the economic and fiscal history of the American states in the last three decades of the twentieth century. It dives deeply into these historical data in search of new insights about the factors that stand behind state economic success.

The Role of Volatility in State Economies and Fiscal Policy

The central point of departure is the elevated role of volatility. This departure from traditional analyses of economic performance tracks the perspective in modern financial theory that emphasizes a two-dimensional, or mean-variance, criterion for evaluating portfolios. Just as rates of return alone provide an incomplete basis for gauging portfolio performance, the level or growth in state economies reveals an incomplete and perhaps distorted picture of performance. Taking the volatility of state economies explicitly into account refines the whole notion of "economic success."

This book explores and illustrates the considerable promise of a two-dimensional or mean-variance criterion for assessing state economic performance. For example, the empirical analysis finds that high-income states tend to be significantly more volatile than low-income states, which raises a host of doubts about the adequacy of traditional models of economic development. Some citizens may simply prefer a low volatility to a high volatility environment, even though this choice requires some sacrifice in the form of residing in a state with below-average income. The mean-variance perspective amends applications of growth models that rely on the mobility of productive factors keyed to income levels alone. The elevated importance of state economic volatility also ushers in novel questions about the determinants of volatility and the interplay between the volatility and the level of state income.

In addition to economic volatility, the book explores and accents the importance of the volatility dimension in state fiscal policy. For example, the analysis of state revenues considers the reliability of alternative tax instruments by computing and comparing the volatility in revenue flows from specific tax sources. Regarding expenditures, the analysis discovers a systematic trade-off between the volatility of state budgets and the efficiency of public sector operations.

Overview of Chapters

The book is organized into 10 chapters. Chapter 1 begins with a review of state economic performance, detailing the variation in living standards and economic growth rates among states. Chapter 2 investigates the pat explanation for the state growth process from neoclassical economics, the "convergence" thesis, which posits that low-income regions will outperform and therefore catch up with the living standards in high-income regions. The appealing simplicity of the neoclassical convergence thesis fails to explain the state experience for at least 25 years; income convergence among the American states ended in the mid-1970s.

Chapter 3 introduces the mean-variance perspective as a positive framework for analyzing state economic performance. Two techniques for computing state economic volatility are developed, and these measures are used to rank and exposit the extent of volatility among states. The chapter surveys alternative theories for an underlying relationship between the level and volatility of state income and probes this relationship empirically. As previewed in the preceding discussion, the statistical models reveal a significant and positive correlation between income and volatility, consistent with the risk-return relationship observed in standard portfolio analysis.

Chapter 4 moves the analysis into the realm of state fiscal policy, specifically beginning with an overview of the evolution of state tax structures. States relied on sales taxes as the predominant revenue source in the 1960s but steadily replaced it with the individual income tax in the succeeding three decades. By the late 1990s, collections from the state income tax were nearly on a par with collections from the sales tax in the typical state. Chapter 5 and chapter 6 proceed to related issues: the progressivity of state tax structures, the impact of income versus sales taxes on economic performance, and the reliability of these alternative revenue sources. The analysis of revenue reliability again brings the role of volatility to the front burner. The results from these analyses help to explain the demise of the state sales tax and its replacement by the income tax. The state sales tax deters economic performance and, contrary to conventional wisdom, provides a less reliable revenue source than the state income tax in almost two-thirds of the states that levy both types of taxes.

Chapter 7 takes up the spending side of fiscal policy, highlighting the wide variation among states over the 1970 through 2000 period. Chapter 8 returns to the mean-variance perspective, in this case applying it to state budget processes. The analysis demonstrates that uncertainty is the enemy of efficiency in public as well as private enterprise. If public budgets are volatile and therefore difficult to predict, agencies incur higher operating costs than if budgets are stable and predictable. State fiscal volatility creates uncertainty that limits the efficiency of agency planning and thereby tends to increase state spending. In light of the elevated importance of fiscal volatility, chapter 8 examines the role of fiscal institutions in a mean-variance perspective. Institutions such as balanced budget requirements, tax and expenditure limitations, biennial budgeting, and the item veto affect fiscal volatility and through this channel have indirect as well as direct effects on the size of government. In essence, fiscal institutions take on a more subtle and significant role in state budgetary processes than previous analyses have appreciated.

Chapter 9 examines the composition of state budgets and the relative influence of various forces in determining spending priorities. The influence of political ideology matters, but not nearly as much as fiscal volatility and fiscal institutions. Chapter 10 reiterates the major results and summarizes the lessons in state political economy that emerge from the study.

Chapter 1

Champions of the State Growth League

The economic history of the United States in the twentieth century reflects enormous progress. Living standards more than quadrupled between 1929, the year of the infamous stock market crash and the beginning of the Great Depression, and 1999. Income per capita rose to just above $29,500 in 1999 from about $7,000 in 1929 (both denominated in 2000 dollars). Figure 1.1 shows the powerful upward trajectory in U.S. living standards over the course of these seven decades.

What dampens the optimism about future economic progress is that the U.S. economy grew at an increasingly slower pace in the closing decades of the twentieth century in comparison to earlier decades. Figure 1.2 illustrates this diminishing performance of the U.S. economy, breaking down the average annual growth rate by decade.[1] In the depression-wracked 1930s real per capita incomes declined slightly, followed by the roaring 1940s, when real per capita income grew at an average annual rate of 3.8 percent. World War II clearly pulled the U.S. economy out of its Great Depression and fueled the best decade of growth in the twentieth century. In the postwar 1950s, growth moderated but remained at a healthy 2.6 percent annual rate before accelerating once again in the 1960s to 3.3 percent. Then came the slowdown: growth rates fell to 1.9 percent in the 1970s, to 1.6 percent in the 1980s, and even lower to 1.3 percent in the 1990s.

A rigorous analysis of the U.S. income data during these seven decades confirms this thesis of a national slowdown. Estimating the regression model specified in equation (1.1) over various subperiods provides a basis for identifying significant differences, both in statistics and in magnitude, in the national income growth rates.

$$\ln (\text{Real Income per Capita}_t) = \text{constant} + \beta (\text{Trend}_t) + \varepsilon_t, \quad (1.1)$$

where ln stands for the natural logarithm, Trend_t stands for a linear time trend, and ε_t represents the regression error term. Using this regression model, the estimated coefficient for β reflects the annual

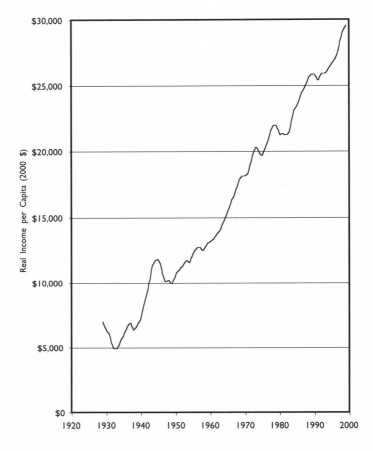

Fig. I.I.   Trajectory of U.S. living standards

growth rate in real per capita income in a given time period. The results of estimating equation (1.1) for the 1929 to 1999 time period
and two subperiods, 1950 to 1999 and 1970 to 1999, are shown in
table 1.1.[2]

The relevant results from the regression analysis in table 1.1 that
test for growth rate declines are summarized in table 1.2. As shown
in the first row, real income per capita grew annually by 3.0 percent
between 1929 and 1969. This growth rate equals exactly twice the 1.5
percent annual growth rate for the 1970 to 1999 period (the difference is significant at the 1 percent confidence level). The estimated
growth rate for the period 1950 to 1969 is 2.6 percent, which is also

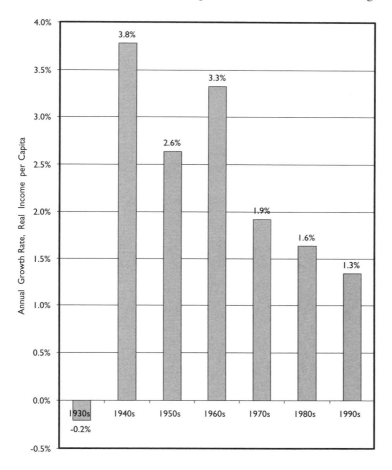

Fig. 1.2.   Decline of U.S. income growth rates in the twentieth century

greater than the 1.5 percent growth rate in the 1970 to 1999 period (this difference is again significant at the 1 percent confidence level). The second row of table 1.2 computes the relative differences in economic growth during these three epochs. The annual growth rate was 100 percent higher in the 1929 to 1969 period compared to the 1970 to 1999 period and was 73 percent higher in the 1950 to 1969 period compared to the 1970 to 1999 period. In short, while the U.S. living standards continued to grow in the last three decades of the twentieth century, this growth slowed significantly compared to the preceding decades.

As a final gauge of the U.S. economic slowdown, table 1.3 presents a simple regression that estimates the growth rate in the last half of the twentieth century. Here the dependent variable is the annual growth rate (continuously compounded), and the dummy variable breaks the sample at its midpoint, equal to zero for the years 1950 through 1974 and equal to one for the years 1975 through 1999. The constant term, 0.027, indicates a growth rate of 2.7 percent in the 1950–74 period, and the dummy variable indicates that the growth rate dropped by 1.2 percentage points in the 1975–99 period. This estimated coefficient on the dummy variable is significant at the 5 percent level, rejecting the thesis that economic growth in the United States remained unchanged over the 50 years.

TABLE 1.1.   U.S. Income Growth Rates, Comparison of Time Periods

Independent Variables	Dependent Variable = ln (Real Income per Capita)[a]		
	1929–99	1950–99	1970–99
Linear time trend	0.030	0.026	0.015
	(15.61)**	(16.61)**	(26.32)**
Post-1969 linear time trend	−0.015	−0.011	—
	(−7.42)**	(−6.64)**	
Dummy variable for World War II years	0.270	—	—
	(6.58)**		
Dummy variable for post-1969 period	0.636	0.507	—
	(9.50)**	(9.28)**	
Constant	8.56	8.69	9.20
	(148.3)**	(191.7)**	(271.7)**
F-statistic	925**	1658**	693**
Number of observations	71	50	30

Note: t-statistics are shown in parentheses.

[a]The dependent variable is entered as a natural logarithmic transformation, denominated in real (2000) dollars. The model estimations use Newey-White standard errors with an AR(1) lag structure.

** Indicates significance at the 1 percent level for a two-tailed test.

TABLE 1.2.   Significant Decline in U.S. Economic Growth

	1929–69[a]	1950–69	1970–99
Income per capita growth rate (in % annualized, real dollars)	3.0	2.6	1.5
Percentage difference in growth rate compared to 1970–99	100	73	

[a]This value excludes the World War II years, which were significantly higher than the other years in the period.

TABLE 1.3.   U.S. Economic Growth Rates in Last Half of the Twentieth Century

Independent Variables	Dependent Variable = Growth Rate in Real Income per Capita, 1950–99[a]
Dummy variable for post-1974 period[b]	−0.012
	(1.97)*
Constant	0.027
	(6.16)**
F-statistic	3.9*
Number of observations	50

Note: t-statistics are shown in parentheses.

[a]The dependent variable is the annual compound growth rate, denominated in real (2000) dollars. The model estimation uses Newey-White standard errors with an AR(1) lag structure.

[b]The dummy variable for the post-1974 period is selected to divide the 50-year sample at its midpoint.

* Indicates significance at the 5 percent level for a two-tailed test. ** Indicates significance at the 1 percent level for a two-tailed test.

The Deceptive Big Picture

These various metrics confirm the conventional wisdom: the aggregate growth rate for the United States began a steady decline in the 1970s that shows no sign of abating at the turn of the twenty-first century. What is less well known is how accurately this aggregate slowdown in U.S. growth characterizes the economic experience of the individual American states. When the model used for table 1.3 is estimated for each of the 50 state economies for the 1950 to 1999 period, an interesting pattern emerges. In only 13 of the states (roughly 1 in 4) do we find a statistically significant decline in the income growth rate using the 5 percent confidence level as the cutoff criterion.[3] If we use a less stringent 10 percent confidence level as the cutoff criterion, we still find a statistically significant drop in economic growth in only 22 states (less than half the nation).[4] Growth rates showed no statistically significant decline in more than half of the states. To put these results another way, the economies of 28 American states departed from the "national" pattern and showed no significant slowdown in the last half of the twentieth century.

With this initial piece of empirical analysis we begin to dispel the notion of the "U.S. economy." The big picture provided by the aggregate data fails to represent adequately the experiences of individual states, and in some cases, as we shall see, the aggregate U.S. data grossly misrepresent state-level circumstances. That major subnational pockets depart from the presumed national picture suggests the importance of state-specific determinants of economic performance.

Traditional Measures of State Economic Performance

To pursue this point further, consider the dissimilarity in economic performance among the American states in the last three decades of the twentieth century. Figure 1.3 ranks the 50 states based on growth rates for the 1969–99 period. The values reflect the average annual growth in real income per capita (using the continuously compounded method described in note 1).

As a benchmark, in the 1970s through the 1990s income per capita for the total United States grew at a 1.63 percent rate using this measurement method, which is close to the growth rate in the median state of 1.69 percent. (Given an even number of American states, Nebraska and Kansas both claim the median position and rank as twenty-fifth and twenty-sixth in fig. 1.3.) North Carolina sits on top of the distribution with an annual growth rate of 2.15 percent. Alaska comes in dead last with a 0.94 percent rate, less than half of the growth rate in North Carolina. Figure 1.3 indicates that many of the fastest growing states tended to be in the South; six of the ten fastest growing states were southern. The slowest growing states tended to be in the West and Midwest.

A casual glance at figure 1.3 shows that state growth rates for the most part ranged between 1.3 percent and 2 percent. This visual inspection comes quite close to a statistical characterization of the data. The range in growth rates represented by the mean value plus and minus one standard deviation is 1.4 percent to 2 percent; two-thirds of the states lie within this range of growth rates. Growth rate differences of less than 1 percentage point might appear trivial, hardly worth notice. Yet, seemingly small growth rate differences yield major economic consequences over time. As a demonstration, compare the historical path of living standards in Missouri and Virginia over these three decades. In 1969, Missouri and Virginia had virtually identical living standards, and both states nearly matched the median income across states in that year ($16,800 in 2000 dollars). Subsequently, Virginia grew at a 2.04 percent annual rate and Missouri grew at a 1.64 annual rate, a difference of 0.4 percentage points. How did their living standards compare 30 years later? In 1999, per capita income rose to $30,809 in Virginia and to $27,196 in Missouri (again in 2000 dollars). Thus, starting with income parity in the late 1960s, Virginia income exceeded Missouri income by $3,500, or 13 percent, in 1999. The lesson, of course, is that seemingly small differences in growth rates pile up

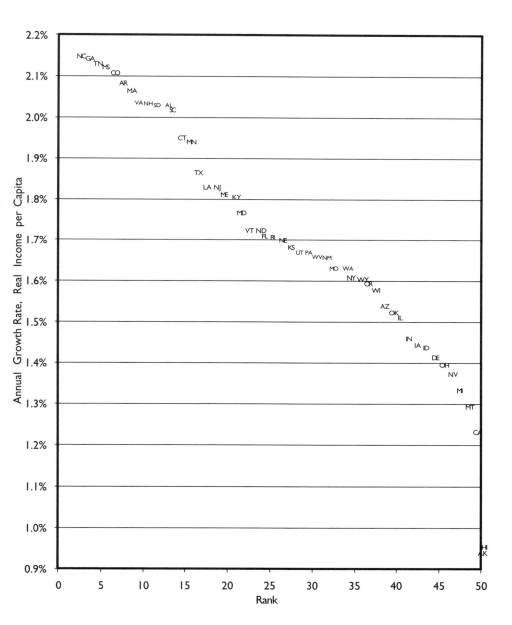

Fig. 1.3. Comparison of state economies, 1969–99 (ranked by growth rate in real income per capita)

and over the years result in meaningful differences in the well-being of the typical family.

Table 1.4 presents state growth estimates using two alternative measurement techniques, the least squares method and the continuously compounded method.[5] The table orders the states from fastest growth (equal to 1) to slowest growth (equal to 50). For comparison, table 1.4 also lists the continuously compounded growth rates (the same values plotted in fig. 1.3) and the state rankings based on that value.

Using the least squares method New Hampshire has the highest growth rate (2.14 percent annually) followed by Connecticut and Massachusetts (2.11 percent). Note that the frequent assertion that the economies of the southern states lead the nation depends upon which growth measure is used. New England states claim the top three spots using the least squares method. In addition, the economic performance of other New England and Mid-Atlantic states ranks considerably higher using the least squares method compared to the continuously compounded method. New Jersey moves into the number 10 spot, and Rhode Island moves into the number 11 spot, whereas these two states appeared near the middle of the pack based on the compound growth metric. New York and Delaware also improve their relative performance rankings substantially. For the United States as a whole income per capita grew at a 1.52 percent rate using the least squares method, right at the growth rate in the median states of 1.51 percent (South Dakota and Missouri). Alaska again finishes last with a 0.33 percent growth rate, which is 85 percent less than New Hampshire's growth rate. Overall, the simple correlation coefficient between the continuously compounded growth rate and the least squares growth rate is 0.86; in other words the two measures are closely, but not perfectly, related.[6]

Figure 1.4 depicts the extensive variation among state economies during the 1969–99 period. This figure provides a frequency distribution, which divides income per capita growth rates into bands of 25 basis points. For example, seven states grew at an annual rate between 1 percent and 1.24 percent, and six states grew at an annual rate between 2 percent and 2.24 percent.

A slightly different way to assess economic performance is to gauge the change in income relative to the change in the state's work force.[7] Figure 1.5 ranks the 50 states based on this indicator. There the values reflect the average annual growth in real income per worker growth rates for the 1969–99 period (using the continuously

TABLE 1.4. State Rankings for Real Income per Capita Growth, 1969-99

	Least Squares Method[a]		Continuously Compounded Method[b]	
	Growth Rate (%)	Rank	Growth Rate (%)	Rank
New Hampshire	2.14	1	2.03	9
Connecticut	2.11	2	1.95	13
Massachusetts	2.11	3	2.07	7
North Carolina	2.10	4	2.15	1
Georgia	2.05	5	2.14	2
Tennessee	2.04	6	2.13	3
Virginia	1.97	7	2.04	8
Alabama	1.91	8	2.03	11
South Carolina	1.90	9	2.02	12
New Jersey	1.89	10	1.83	17
Rhode Island	1.79	11	1.71	24
Mississippi	1.79	12	2.12	4
Arkansas	1.78	13	2.08	6
Maine	1.77	14	1.81	18
Vermont	1.75	15	1.73	21
Minnesota	1.74	16	1.94	14
Colorado	1.70	17	2.11	5
Maryland	1.69	18	1.77	20
New York	1.67	19	1.61	33
Florida	1.63	20	1.71	23
Louisiana	1.62	21	1.83	16
Kentucky	1.62	22	1.81	19
Pennsylvania	1.59	23	1.67	28
Texas	1.53	24	1.87	15
South Dakota	1.53	25	2.03	10
Missouri	1.50	26	1.63	31
Washington	1.48	27	1.63	32
Nebraska	1.46	28	1.70	25
Delaware	1.43	29	1.41	43
New Mexico	1.42	30	1.66	30
Wisconsin	1.37	31	1.58	36
Kansas	1.35	32	1.68	26
Indiana	1.35	33	1.46	40
Illinois	1.34	34	1.51	39
West Virginia	1.34	35	1.66	29
Ohio	1.33	36	1.40	44
Oregon	1.32	37	1.59	35
Utah	1.30	38	1.67	27
Arizona	1.28	39	1.54	37
Michigan	1.25	40	1.33	46
Oklahoma	1.23	41	1.52	38
Iowa	1.18	42	1.44	41
Nevada	1.15	43	1.37	45
Idaho	1.13	44	1.44	42
California	1.09	45	1.23	48
Hawaii	1.01	46	0.96	49
North Dakota	1.00	47	1.72	22
Wyoming	0.95	48	1.61	34
Montana	0.88	49	1.29	47
Alaska	0.33	50	0.94	50

[a]The least squares method uses the regression model specified in equation (1.2a) in note 5.
[b]The continuously compounded method uses the formula shown in note 1.

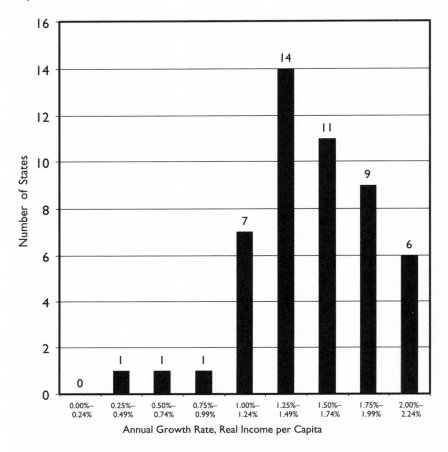

Fig. 1.4.   Distribution of state growth rates, 1969–99

compounded method described in note 1). As a benchmark, in the 1970s through the 1990s income per worker for the entire United States grew at a 0.67 percent rate using this measurement method, which exactly equals the median growth rate per worker among states. (Missouri and Illinois occupy the median position in fig. 1.5.) North Carolina returns as the growth champion, with an annual growth rate of 1.28 percent. Alaska finally moves out of the cellar, replaced by Montana, which experienced an annual growth rate in income per worker of 0.04 percent. Figure 1.5 places eight southern states among the top ten in terms of income per worker growth; all of the bottom ten states are from the Midwest and West.

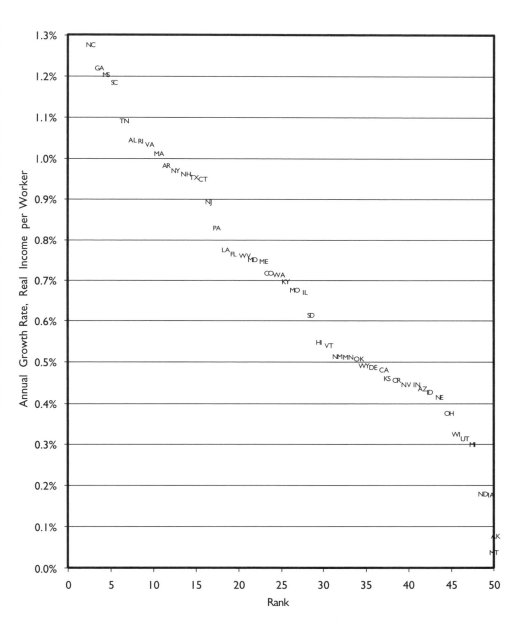

Fig. 1.5. Comparison of state economies, 1969–99 (ranked by growth rate in real income per worker)

Table 1.5 ranks the states based on growth in real income per worker. Based on the least squares method, North Carolina, the leader, has a growth rate of 1.12 percent, followed by South Carolina (1.09 percent) and Georgia (1.03 percent). Five states experienced negative growth in income per worker: North Dakota, Alaska, Montana, Iowa, and Utah. Income per worker remained unchanged in Wyoming over the three decades.

It is important to note that the growth rates in income per worker run much lower than the growth rates in income per capita. The median growth rate in income per worker is 0.43 percent, compared to the 1.51 percent median growth rate in income per capita. This difference reflects the fact that labor force growth outstripped population growth by a wide margin. The rise of the proportion of women who worked outside the home during these three decades accounts for most of this demographic shift. Also noteworthy are some significant changes in how particular states' rankings differ under the alternative growth metrics. Mississippi provides a telling example. Gauging performance in terms of income per worker growth, Mississippi ranks fifth (using the least squares method in table 1.5), whereas it ranks twelfth in terms of income per capita growth (table 1.4). Florida ranks a respectable fourteenth in terms of per worker growth, whereas it ranks a mediocre twentieth in terms of per capita growth. California ranks twenty-ninth in per worker growth, fairly near the median value, whereas it ranks forty-fifth in terms of per capita growth. Finally, with regard to the income per worker measures, the simple correlation between the continuously compounded growth rate and the least squares growth rate is 0.95, indicating that these two measures yield quite consistent performance rankings.

The Dispersion of State Living Standards

The analysis now turns to a second performance measure, the level of real income, which is the traditional indicator used to assess living standards. First, table 1.6 ranks the states based on the level of real income per capita. Per capita incomes and state rankings are shown for two four-year intervals, 1996–99 and 1969–72. Here the analysis uses the four-year average for each state at the beginning and the end of the period to dampen the importance of a random downturn or upturn that may have occurred in a single year. However, comparing the state income rankings in 1999 to 1969 yields basically similar results.

At the close of the twentieth century (the 1996–99 period), real per capita income in the median state (Oregon and Kansas) equaled

TABLE 1.5. State Rankings for Real Income per Worker Growth, 1969–99

	Least Squares Method[a]		Continuously Compounded Method[b]	
	Growth Rate (%)	Rank	Growth Rate (%)	Rank
North Carolina	1.12	1	1.28	1
South Carolina	1.09	2	1.19	4
Georgia	1.03	3	1.22	2
Connecticut	0.99	4	0.95	14
Mississippi	0.98	5	1.20	3
Rhode Island	0.97	6	1.04	7
Tennessee	0.92	7	1.09	5
New York	0.92	8	0.97	11
Massachusetts	0.91	9	1.01	9
Virginia	0.89	10	1.03	8
Alabama	0.86	11	1.04	6
New Hampshire	0.86	12	0.96	12
New Jersey	0.82	13	0.89	15
Florida	0.73	14	0.77	18
Pennsylvania	0.70	15	0.83	16
Texas	0.68	16	0.95	13
Louisiana	0.67	17	0.78	17
Arkansas	0.63	18	0.98	10
Maine	0.56	19	0.75	21
Maryland	0.56	20	0.75	20
West Virginia	0.52	21	0.76	19
Kentucky	0.49	22	0.70	24
Missouri	0.47	23	0.68	25
Illinois	0.44	24	0.67	26
Hawaii	0.44	25	0.55	28
Delaware	0.43	26	0.49	34
Colorado	0.36	27	0.72	22
Vermont	0.36	28	0.54	29
California	0.35	29	0.48	35
Nevada	0.34	30	0.45	38
Oklahoma	0.33	31	0.51	32
Washington	0.31	32	0.71	23
New Mexico	0.29	33	0.51	30
Minnesota	0.29	34	0.51	31
Ohio	0.26	35	0.38	43
Indiana	0.21	36	0.45	39
Oregon	0.20	37	0.46	37
Nebraska	0.19	38	0.42	42
Idaho	0.18	39	0.43	41
Arizona	0.18	40	0.44	40
Kansas	0.17	41	0.46	36
Wisconsin	0.11	42	0.32	44
Michigan	0.09	43	0.30	46
South Dakota	0.09	44	0.61	27
Wyoming	0.00	45	0.49	33
Utah	−0.01	46	0.32	45
Iowa	−0.06	47	0.18	48
Montana	−0.30	48	0.04	50
Alaska	−0.36	49	0.08	49
North Dakota	−0.43	50	0.18	47

[a]The least squares method uses the regression model specified in equation (1.2b) in note 5.
[b]The continuously compounded method uses the formula shown in note 1.

TABLE 1.6. State Rankings Based on Real Income per Capita (in 2000 $)

	1996–99[a]		1969–72[b]	
	Income per Capita	Rank	Income per Capita	Rank
Connecticut	$38,964	1	$22,843	2
New Jersey	35,368	2	21,816	6
Massachusetts	34,547	3	20,225	11
New York	33,499	4	22,039	5
Maryland	32,038	5	20,669	10
Illinois	30,996	6	20,799	9
Nevada	30,906	7	22,077	4
Colorado	30,740	8	18,454	15
New Hampshire	30,473	9	17,636	23
Minnesota	30,336	10	18,247	18
Delaware	30,322	11	20,967	8
Washington	29,541	12	19,008	13
California	29,382	13	21,640	7
Virginia	29,378	14	17,360	30
Alaska	29,194	15	23,445	1
Rhode Island	29,028	16	18,432	16
Pennsylvania	28,451	17	18,393	17
Hawaii	28,265	18	22,532	3
Florida	27,955	19	18,141	19
Michigan	27,918	20	19,421	12
Wisconsin	27,121	21	18,062	20
Ohio	27,110	22	18,602	14
Georgia	27,032	23	15,535	37
Nebraska	27,026	24	17,451	26
Oregon	26,995	25	17,932	22
Kansas	26,550	26	17,558	24
Texas	26,448	27	16,428	31
Missouri	26,396	28	17,388	29
North Carolina	26,341	29	14,975	41
Indiana	26,027	30	17,541	25
Wyoming	25,856	31	17,946	21
Iowa	25,804	32	17,439	27
Vermont	25,624	33	16,412	32
Tennessee	25,523	34	14,614	42
Arizona	24,928	35	17,389	28
South Dakota	24,702	36	15,079	40
Maine	24,401	37	15,287	39
North Dakota	23,413	38	15,559	36
South Carolina	23,380	39	13,911	47
Kentucky	23,136	40	14,455	44
Utah	23,060	41	15,393	38
Louisiana	23,060	42	14,091	46
Alabama	23,032	43	13,610	48
Oklahoma	22,996	44	15,700	35
Idaho	22,880	45	16,059	34
Arkansas	22,128	46	13,046	49
Montana	22,048	47	16,392	33
New Mexico	22,014	48	14,499	43
West Virginia	21,047	49	14,129	45
Mississippi	20,647	50	12,110	50

[a]Figures use the mean value in real income per capita for the years 1996 through 1999, in 2000 dollars.

[b]Figures use the mean value in real income per capita for the years 1969 through 1972, in 2000 dollars.

$26,773 and ranged from $38,964 in Connecticut to $20,647 in Mississippi, a spread of almost two to one. Alaska topped the rankings and Mississippi bottomed the rankings in the 1969–72 period, and there again the income spread was about two to one. While the proportionate distance between the richest and poorest states remained about the same, the pecking order in living standards was substantially reshuffled. Starting at the extremes, among the ten states at the bottom of the income ladder in the 1969–72 period, four had climbed out by the 1996–99 period (South Carolina, Tennessee, North Carolina, and South Dakota). Among the ten richest states in the 1969–72 period, four had fallen out of this coveted category by the end of the twentieth century (Alaska, Hawaii, California, and Delaware).

Table 1.7 further displays the considerable dispersion in the state incomes, assessed this time in terms of the level of real income per worker. These results follow the format used in table 1.6, reporting the mean per worker income levels and state rankings at the beginning and end of the three decades. Based on this indicator of living standards, New Jersey and Connecticut topped the rankings at the beginning and at the end of these three decades. North Dakota and Montana ranked lowest in the 1996–99 period, replacing South Carolina and Mississippi, which had the lowest incomes per worker in the 1969–72 period. Among the poorest ten states by this ranking, seven changed between 1969–72 and 1996–99. Among the ten richest states, three fell from grace during these three decades.

Figure 1.6 provides a visual look at these relative state income data using income per capita as the performance indicator. The layout in figure 1.6 indicates the extent to which the relative well-being among the states remained constant over the 1969–99 period. The states' rankings in terms of income per capita in the late 1960s to early 1970s period are shown on the vertical axis, and the states' rankings in the late 1990s are shown on the horizontal axis. The richest state ranks as 1, and the poorest state ranks as 50. This setup easily identifies those states whose relative economic conditions remained unchanged over these three decades; such states will fall along the 45 degree line in figure 1.6. For example, Mississippi ranks as the poorest state throughout the three decades. Only three other states maintained the same relative income per capita ranking: Rhode Island, Pennsylvania, and Florida.

The distance to the left of the 45 degree line indicates the extent to which a state's income per capita improved relative to other states. Virginia tops the list of outperforming states over the period, followed

TABLE I.7. State Rankings Based on Real Income per Worker (in 2000 $)

	1996–99[a]		1969–72[b]	
	Income per Worker	Rank	Income per Worker	Rank
New Jersey	$63,006	1	$50,487	1
Connecticut	62,421	2	49,328	2
New York	60,677	3	47,871	5
Maryland	55,706	4	47,717	7
Massachusetts	53,893	5	43,210	10
Illinois	52,185	6	45,106	8
California	52,164	7	47,832	6
Rhode Island	51,107	8	39,953	21
Pennsylvania	50,756	9	41,705	16
Florida	50,448	10	41,746	15
Michigan	50,381	11	47,919	4
Washington	49,289	12	43,508	9
New Hampshire	48,550	13	39,207	24
Virginia	47,627	14	37,340	29
Delaware	47,269	15	41,805	14
Nevada	47,010	16	43,013	11
Alaska	46,722	17	48,242	3
Ohio	45,822	18	42,459	12
Texas	45,222	19	36,489	33
Hawaii	45,031	20	40,362	19
Georgia	44,788	21	33,496	43
Arizona	44,744	22	41,815	13
Colorado	44,742	23	39,472	23
Minnesota	44,690	24	40,578	18
West Virginia	43,868	25	37,425	28
Oregon	43,620	26	40,170	20
Indiana	43,234	27	39,513	22
Louisiana	43,184	28	35,795	38
Wisconsin	42,862	29	40,768	17
Alabama	42,456	30	33,146	44
Missouri	42,302	31	36,899	31
North Carolina	42,163	32	30,828	48
Tennessee	41,411	33	31,832	46
Kansas	40,874	34	38,293	25
South Carolina	40,869	35	30,297	49
Kentucky	40,867	36	34,840	40
New Mexico	40,656	37	36,601	32
Maine	40,528	38	34,596	41
Oklahoma	39,823	39	35,866	36
Vermont	39,336	40	35,849	37
Iowa	39,286	41	38,066	26
Wyoming	39,281	42	36,997	30
Mississippi	39,123	43	29,151	50
Nebraska	39,039	44	36,068	34
Arkansas	38,732	45	30,932	47
Idaho	38,459	46	35,639	39
Utah	36,942	47	35,998	35
South Dakota	36,209	48	33,079	45
Montana	35,957	49	37,724	27
North Dakota	34,002	50	34,451	42

[a]Figures use the mean value in real income per worker for the years 1994 through 1997, in 2000 dollars.

[b]Figures use the mean value in real income per worker for the years 1969 through 1972, in 2000 dollars.

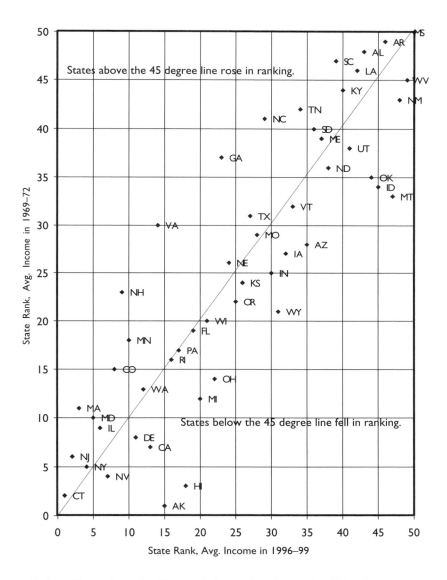

Fig. 1.6. Changes in relative living standards over three decades (1 = highest income per capita; 50 = lowest income per capita)

by New Hampshire, Georgia, North Carolina, Massachusetts, Minnesota, Tennessee, and South Carolina. The extent to which a state lost ground in relation to other states is gauged in figure 1.6 by the distance to the right of the 45 degree line. The biggest losers are Hawaii, Montana, Alaska, Idaho, Wyoming, Oklahoma, Ohio, and Michigan. The fate of several of these state economies is clearly tied to the decline in oil and gas prices. The correlation between the states' incomes per capita at the beginning and end of the period is 0.84, and correlation in the states' rankings is 0.88.

Figure 1.7 illustrates the dispersion in living standards based on the results of the level of income per worker. The two richest states by this measure, New Jersey and Connecticut, maintained dominance throughout the period. The rankings of only two other states remained unchanged, Colorado and Missouri. Topping the list of gainers are Georgia, North Carolina, Virginia, Texas, Alabama, South Carolina, Rhode Island, and Tennessee. Clearly southern states dominate the group of most-improved states by this performance indicator. Again in figure 1.7 the distance to the left of the 45 degree line depicts the strength of a state's increase in relative income status. The distance to the right of the 45 degree line depicts the strength of a state's decrease in relative income status. In terms of the income per worker indicator, Montana heads the list of underperformers, followed by Iowa, Alaska, Utah, Wyoming, Wisconsin, Nebraska, Kansas, Arizona, and North Dakota. The farm states of the Midwest are obviously overrepresented in this group of underperforming states. The correlation between the states' income per worker at the beginning and end of the period is 0.81, and the correlation in the ranks is 0.79.

The results summarized in figures 1.6 and 1.7 indicate considerable differences among states in changes in living standards over these decades. Rather than revealing a consistent secular rise in incomes that affected all states relatively evenly, the data reveal that economic performance widely varied in terms of relative income gains and losses.

Commentary

Every fall the Virginia Governor's Advisory Board of Economists convenes in Richmond for its annual task of forecasting the state's three-year economic outlook. The board's economic forecasts nail down the main parameters used to project future tax revenues and therefore the available resources for the governor's proposed state

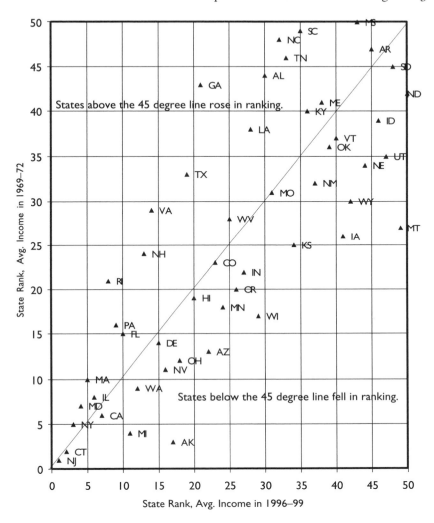

Fig. 1.7.   Changes in relative living standards over three decades (1 = highest income per worker; 50 = lowest income per worker)

budget. Like many states, Virginia's forecasting process starts with a forecast for the U.S. economy, with projections for the national growth rate in such factors as income, employment, corporate earnings, and inflation. These national projections drive the state's econometric models, a so-called top-down forecasting process. This conventional process of state economic and fiscal forecasting, while reasonable, glosses over a major fact: Virginia's economy bears little resemblance to the "national" economy. In the last three decades of the twentieth century Virginia's economy increased nearly 30 percent faster than the U.S. economy.

The enormous variety in the economic experiences of the American states does not yield easily to the construct of a national U.S. economy. The evidence using traditional measures of economic growth and living standards indicates that state economies march to disparate beats. Even the often-voiced "fact" of a U.S. economic slowdown fails to capture the reality in over half of the states.

This overview of state economic developments during the twentieth century and especially during the closing three decades lays the framework for the analysis in subsequent chapters. There the focus is on the extent to which the mobility of productive resources, economic volatility, and specific fiscal policies affect the course of state economic events.

Chapter 2

The End of State Income Convergence

The convergence thesis offers a broad and plausible explanation for the widely different rates of state economic development that chapter 1 describes. The most important feature behind the convergence thesis as it applies to the American states is the free flow of productive resources and ideas across state lines. In a market economy with open borders such as in the American states, workers, physical capital, technology, and knowledge have practically unlimited mobility. Freedom of mobility means that productive resources will relocate into areas where profit opportunities arise. Resource mobility should ensure that, in the long run, wages and rates of return on investments would be equalized among regions.

For example, if wages or rates of return are lower in one state than in another, workers and firms face clear incentives to relocate. Labor migration drives wages up and rates of return down in the states that lose workers, and it drives wages down and rates of return up in the states that receive the migrants. Likewise, technology, knowledge, and physical capital flow readily across state borders. If a technological innovation raises productivity in one area, profit-motivated firms in other areas eventually adopt the innovation. In this framework, long-term growth is predominantly determined by demographic and technological factors. Given the same resources and access to technology as well as mobile productive factors, states should converge to a common long-run, steady-state level of income per worker.[1]

Empirical analyses of the convergence thesis focus on two types of evidence. First, convergence implies a narrowing in the dispersion of income among states over time. As labor migrates from low-wage to high-wage states and capital flows from high-wage to low-wage states, poor states predictably grow faster than rich states, thereby closing the income gap between rich and poor states.[2]

Figure 2.1 examines the income dispersion pattern in the American states from 1929 through 1999. The graph plots the coefficient of variation in the log of real income per capita across states for each

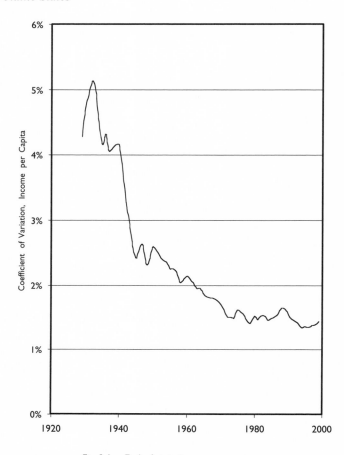

Fig. 2.1.   End of state income convergence

year, the appropriate measure to compare dispersion over time.[3] A decline in the coefficient of variation indicates convergence (a narrowing in income differences among states), and an increase in the coefficient of variation indicates divergence (a widening in income differences). As illustrated in figure 2.1, income per capita across states strongly converged between 1930 and the mid-1940s. A slower rate of convergence appears between the mid-1940s and the mid-1970s. The dispersion among the states oscillated within a fairly narrow range until the late 1970s and then diverged until the late 1980s. Convergence reappears in the early 1990s and ends in 1994. It is important to note that the dispersion in income per capita in 1999 was roughly the same as it was 25 years earlier.

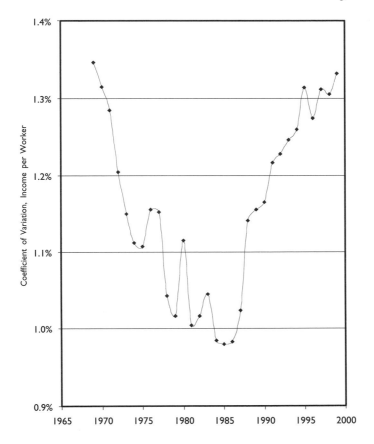

Fig. 2.2.   Pattern of convergence in state income per worker

The evidence indicating an end to state income convergence is
even stronger using data on real income per worker. As shown in
figure 2.2, the coefficient of variation in income per worker generally
converged between 1969 and 1979, oscillated with a narrow range
until the mid-1980s, and then diverged sharply for the remaining
data series (through 1999). These two indicators of the dispersion of
income among states weigh against the view that the state growth
process, at least in the last three decades of the twentieth century, is
an exogenous, automatic process driven principally by income gaps
that encourage factor migration.[4]

Barro and Sala-i-Martin (1992, 1995) and Barro (1991, 1997) offered a series of articles and books that popularized the second test

of the convergence thesis. These works examined both American state and international data.[5] This test uses the regression model specified in equation (2.1):

$$\text{Income Growth}_i = \beta \ln (\text{Initial Income})_i + \text{Constant} + \varepsilon_i. \quad (2.1)$$

Income Growth$_i$ is the annual growth rate in real per capita income in state i over a particular period. The independent variable, ln (Initial Income)$_i$, measures the natural logarithm of real income per capita at the beginning of the period in state i. ε_i is the regression error term.

The logic of the Barro-type regression test of the convergence hypothesis is straightforward. If high-income states grow faster than low-income states, we expect a significantly negative sign on the estimated coefficient for β. The results are reported in table 2.1 for four models that use the alternative measures of state growth described in chapter 1. These state growth rates are measured for the years 1969 through 1999, the period that income convergence appears to have ended based on the patterns in figures 2.1 and 2.2.[6]

The first two columns in table 2.1 use the growth in real income

TABLE 2.1.   Barro-Type Test for State Income Convergence, 1969–99

Independent Variables	Growth in Income per Capita		Growth in Income per Worker	
	Continuously Compounded[a]	Least Squares[b]	Continuously Compounded[a]	Least Squares[b]
ln (Initial Income)	−0.009	−0.005	−0.007	−0.004
	(−3.85)**	(−1.38)	(−2.08)*	(−0.94)
Constant	0.104	0.063	0.080	0.049
	(4.61)**	(1.83)	(2.26)*	(1.04)
R-squared	0.27	0.05	0.10	0.02
F-statistic	14.71**	1.92	4.31*	0.88
Number of observations	50	50	50	50

Note: *t*-statistics are shown in parentheses.

[a]The continuously compounded growth rate is computed as $[\ln(X_{1999}/X_{1969})] / 30$, where ln is the natural logarithm, X_{1999} is real income in 1999, X_{1969} is real income in 1969, and 30 is the number of years in the sample.

[b]The least squares growth rate is computed by regressing the natural logarithm of income in each state on a linear time trend as follows:

$$\ln (\text{Real Income per Capita}_t) = \text{Constant} + \beta_{ypc} (\text{Time Trend}_{1969-99}) + u_t,$$
$$\ln (\text{Real Income per Worker}_t) = \text{Constant} + \beta_{ypw} (\text{Time Trend}_{1969-99}) + u_t,$$

where ln refers to the natural logarithm, the subscript t refers to the value in each year, and u_t is the random error term. In this specification the estimated coefficients for β_{ypc} and β_{ypw} yield the annual growth rates.

* Indicates significance at the 5 percent level for a two-tailed test. ** Indicates significance at the 1 percent level for a two-tailed test.

per capita, and the second two columns use the growth in real income per worker. In both pairs of results, the two alternative measures of growth are examined, one computed by the continuously compounded method and the other by the least squares method.

The findings from the regression models provide conflicting evidence with respect to the income convergence thesis. The estimated coefficient for β is negative and significant in the two models that use the continuously compounded growth rate in income. However, in the two models that use the least squares growth rate, the estimated coefficient for β is not significantly different from zero. At this point the seemingly excessive attention to measurement issues becomes highly relevant. The studies by Watson (1992) and Easterly and Rebelo (1993) stress that the least squares growth rate is more robust to differences in the serial correlation properties of the data than the geometric or continuously compounded rate of growth. In other words, the only Barro-type model that supports the convergence thesis appears to be an artifact of the way the growth rate is measured. At a minimum, the findings in table 2.1 reveal that such evidence is not robust with respect to how one calibrates growth.

Commentary

The abrupt end to the process of income convergence in the American states begs explanation. In a neoclassical growth framework, regional income differences reflect opportunities that would encourage workers and firms to relocate in search of higher living standards and returns on investments. Why would these wealth-increasing opportunities remain untaken with open state borders and relatively low costs of relocation? One possibility is simply that such opportunities are too small to motivate further factor migration. That is, the convergence process petered out when the income differential among states fell to a point where it roughly equaled the costs of relocating. In essence, the geographic distribution of income among states reached equilibrium in the mid-1970s. A quick glance at the state income data in tables 1.6 and 1.7 casts doubt on this explanation. These data point to a number of interstate moves by which a worker could potentially increase his or her income by 20 percent or more. Such potential income gains would seem to exceed the cost of relocating.

Other possible explanations for the stalling of state income convergence lie in alternative growth theories. For example, the increasing returns to the knowledge model advanced by Paul Romer (1986) or the core-perimeter model by Krugman (1991) predict regional disparities in income and income growth rates that can persist for extended periods.[7] The absence of convergence clearly raises the potential relevance of such models to the modern state experience.

Subsequent chapters remain more or less within the neoclassical growth framework, with extensions and modifications that seem to account for the American state experience. Chapter 3 pursues the idea that factor migration is not driven solely by income differences; assessments of state economic risks play a significant role. Chapter 4 pursues the economic consequences of state fiscal policy. The basic idea is simply that tax policies determine after-tax incomes and rates of return and that after-tax differences among the states provide the relevant market signals. In other words, the standard neoclassical model of economic growth attributes most of long-term growth to the automatic forces of convergence. However, state policies exert an impact on that process by affecting underlying payoffs to productive factors.

Chapter 3

Volatile States: Estimates of the Risk-Return Trade-Off

Assessments of macroeconomic performance normally rely on indicators such as income per capita, output per capita, and employment levels or the growth rates of these indicators. The sorts of measures described and analyzed in chapter 1 are typical of the standards used to gauge state economic performance. From the standpoint of modern financial theory, however, such measures tell only part of the performance story.

Suppose Portfolio A yields a 10 percent rate of return and Portfolio B yields a 5 percent rate of return. Would investors prefer Portfolio A or Portfolio B? The answer, of course, is uncertain. An assessment is not possible without information about the risk associated with Portfolio A and Portfolio B and without information about the risk preferences of individual investors. Modern financial theory relies on a two-dimensional criterion to evaluate and explain asset performance: the risk as well as the rate of return.[1]

This chapter examines the volatility of state economies and seeks to flesh out the two-dimensional approach to assessing macroeconomic performance. Comparing the economies of California and New York previews how this approach changes tradition assessments. In America's two largest states, income per worker and income per capita were almost identical in 1970. By 1999, income per worker was 15 percent higher in New York than in California (a difference of nearly $8,000 per worker), and income per capita was 14 percent higher in New York than in California (about $4,200 per capita). Did the New York economy outperform the California economy over these three decades? By traditional measures, New York is the clear winner. By analogy to portfolio theory, the answer depends on the relative risk, or volatility, experienced in these two states. As the measures developed in this chapter indicate, the volatility of income per worker in New York exceeded volatility in California by 60 percent. The volatility of income per capita in New York exceeded volatility in California by 25 percent. In essence, focusing on income levels alone reveals an incomplete and, in this case, a misleading picture. A high-income, high-volatility economy (New York) may or may not be preferable to another with lower income and lower volatility (California). Returning to the portfolio perspective, the 15 percent income differential may reflect a risk premium for residing in New York instead of California.

This chapter introduces the two-dimension perspective first by computing several indices to gauge state economic volatility. How the states fare with respect to these volatility indices is then described. Finally, the chapter analyzes both theoretically and empirically the relationship between levels of economic activity and the volatility of state economies.

The Volatility of State Economies: Measures and Comparisons

The usual statistical tool used to measure volatility is a standard deviation. At least three cross-national studies measure volatility as the standard deviation in a nation's annual growth rates over time (Kormendi and McGuire 1985; Grier and Tullock 1989; Ramey and Ramey 1995). Ramey and Ramey (1995) raise potential drawbacks to this measure of economic volatility and propose two alternative approaches. The first relies on residuals from a core regression model that controls for other important factors that explain changes in macroeconomic conditions. One objection to this measure is that it includes both the predictable and the unpredictable income fluctuations. They propose an alternative that comes closer to capturing the unpredictable element in economic fluctuations; this measure uses variations in the residuals from a time-series forecasting equation. Both approaches to the measurement of state economic volatility are employed subsequently.

The measurement and subsequent analysis of state economic volatility focus on the volatility in levels of economic activity, specifically fluctuations in income per capita and income per worker. This departs from the cross-country studies noted earlier that focus on the volatility in growth rates. Of course, this distinction is important. The decision to analyze levels rather than growth rates follows from the underlying theoretical framework. As discussed later in the chapter, a link between volatility and income levels is easier to establish on conceptual grounds than is a link between volatility and income growth rates.[2]

The first measure of state economic volatility is computed in two steps, beginning by estimating the model specified in equation (3.1).

$$\ln \text{(Income per Capita}_{it}) = \Phi X_{it} + \text{Constant} + \varepsilon_{it}. \tag{3.1}$$

The data sample used to estimate equation (3.1) pools time-series and cross-sectional data; the variable subscript i denotes an observation on an individual state, and the subscript t denotes an observation in a particular year. The dependent variable, ln (Income per Capita$_{it}$), is the natural logarithm of annual income in state i in year t (adjusted for inflation using 2000 prices as the base year) divided by population in state i in year t. Equation (3.1) is estimated as a cross-sectional time-series linear (or panel) model using a feasible generalized least squares (FGLS) technique. The specific procedure used iterates the GLS estimation technique to convergence. The FGLS technique allows estimation in the presence of autocorrelation within states and cross-sectional heteroskedasticity across states.[3]

X_{it} represents a vector of variables that control for basic factors expected to influence state income. These variables include the education level of the populations, state size (i.e., population), the percentage of the population residing in urban areas, and the percentage of the population between the ages of 17 and 65.[4] As mentioned, the model estimation assumes first-order autocorrelation within states and estimates a state-specific coefficient of the AR(1) process.

The sample for estimating equation (3.1) includes all 50 states for the years 1969 through 1999. Table 3.A1 in the appendix at the end of this chapter provides summary statistics for the variables and data sources. Table 3.1 shows the estimated results using two dependent variables, Income per Capita (Model 1) and Income per Worker (Model 2).

The second step in measuring state economic volatility computes the standard deviation of ε_{it}, the residuals from the models estimated using equation (3.1). That is, these residuals represent the deviations in Income per Capita (or Income per Worker) from the values predicted based on the variables in X_{it}. Again two metrics are computed, one using the residuals from the Income per Capita equation (Model 1 in table 3.1) and the other using the residuals from the Income per Worker equation (Model 2 in table 3.1).

Table 3.2 presents the values obtained from this measurement procedure for each state under the column labeled "Regression." Table 3.2 also presents the state rankings based on this measure, where the state with the least volatility receives a rank of 1 and the state with the most volatility receives a rank of 50. Before discussing these findings in detail, the second method of measuring volatility will be described.

One potential limitation of this Regression Volatility measure is that it includes both the predictable and the unpredictable fluctuations in state economies. As an alternative measure Ramey and Ramey (1995) suggest computing the standard deviation in "innovations" in income from a time-series forecasting equation. The idea behind this second approach is that fluctuations in unexpected income correspond more closely to actual uncertainty about the economy than do fluctuations correlated with, say, a state's demographic composition. In other words, anticipated changes in the economy allow firms, workers, policymakers, and consumers to plan and adjust their choices appropriately. When the economy deviates from its expected path, plans get disrupted and productive activities require costly adjustments; for example, an unanticipated downturn in the economy distorts performance even more than an anticipated downturn.

The second measure of state economic volatility that incorporates this notion of uncertainty is the standard deviation in the error term (ε_t) using the time-series regression model shown in equation (3.2):

$$\ln (\text{Income per Capita}_t) = \text{constant} + \beta\,(\text{Year}_t) + \varepsilon_t, \qquad (3.2)$$

TABLE 3.1.   Core Variables Used to Explain State Income, 1969–99

Independent Variables	Dependent Variable = Income per Capita[a] Model 1	Dependent Variable = Income per Worker[a] Model 2
Education (% of population, BA or higher)[b]	0.057 (28.52)**	0.009 (12.10)**
ln (Population)	−0.015 (−2.48)**	0.004 (0.94)
Urban Population (% of population)[b]	0.003 (10.32)**	0.003 (15.45)*
Population Age 18 to 64 (% of population)[b]	0.016 (9.93)**	0.008 (6.48)**
Constant	8.659 (82.44)**	9.754 (119.23)**
Wald chi-squared	3343**	1316**
Total panel observations	1,550	1,550

Note: z-statistics are shown in parentheses.
[a]Variables entered as natural logarithmic transformations, denominated in real (2000) dollars.
[b]Variables denominated as fractions are multiplied by 100 in the estimation models.
* Indicates significance at the 5 percent level for a two-tailed test. ** Indicates significance at the 1 percent level for a two-tailed test.

TABLE 3.2. Economic Volatility Measures by State, 1969–99

	Volatility in Income per Capita				Volatility in Income per Worker			
	Regression[a]	Rank	Innovation[b]	Rank	Regression[a]	Rank	Innovation[b]	Rank
Alabama	0.051	27	0.032	10	0.034	14	0.029	27
Alaska	0.115	50	0.110	50	0.087	49	0.060	49
Arizona	0.037	12	0.035	17	0.035	16	0.019	2
Arkansas	0.059	41	0.039	32	0.040	23	0.042	43
California	0.039	15	0.037	26	0.033	13	0.022	11
Colorado	0.037	13	0.029	5	0.046	30	0.025	19
Connecticut	0.060	42	0.040	35	0.065	45	0.043	44
Delaware	0.052	30	0.036	23	0.024	3	0.018	1
Florida	0.056	38	0.032	9	0.036	18	0.021	8
Georgia	0.054	33	0.035	19	0.041	24	0.025	20
Hawaii	0.061	43	0.041	38	0.036	17	0.027	24
Idaho	0.053	31	0.044	42	0.039	22	0.027	23
Illinois	0.051	28	0.033	13	0.029	9	0.022	13
Indiana	0.054	32	0.037	29	0.032	11	0.023	15
Iowa	0.056	39	0.044	43	0.072	46	0.036	42
Kansas	0.039	14	0.035	18	0.053	40	0.028	26
Kentucky	0.035	10	0.030	7	0.027	7	0.028	25
Louisiana	0.032	5	0.042	41	0.024	4	0.026	22
Maine	0.043	20	0.040	37	0.032	12	0.030	30
Maryland	0.055	35	0.037	25	0.059	42	0.026	21
Massachusetts	0.055	36	0.045	44	0.059	43	0.047	47
Michigan	0.050	26	0.042	40	0.044	28	0.023	16
Minnesota	0.049	25	0.034	16	0.060	44	0.029	29
Mississippi	0.055	34	0.037	27	0.048	33	0.033	35
Missouri	0.032	6	0.026	1	0.025	5	0.021	9
Montana	0.055	37	0.041	39	0.078	48	0.035	39
Nebraska	0.043	19	0.035	20	0.053	36	0.031	34
Nevada	0.072	47	0.039	33	0.048	32	0.036	41
New Hampshire	0.048	23	0.051	46	0.037	19	0.030	32
New Jersey	0.039	17	0.034	14	0.043	27	0.031	33
New Mexico	0.028	2	0.028	3	0.028	8	0.022	14
New York	0.049	24	0.038	30	0.050	34	0.035	37
North Carolina	0.068	46	0.035	21	0.053	39	0.024	18
North Dakota	0.107	49	0.094	49	0.137	50	0.093	50
Ohio	0.034	8	0.029	4	0.031	10	0.020	6
Oklahoma	0.028	1	0.046	45	0.034	15	0.035	38
Oregon	0.043	18	0.040	36	0.038	21	0.021	7
Pennsylvania	0.035	9	0.027	2	0.026	6	0.020	5
Rhode Island	0.044	21	0.037	28	0.053	37	0.033	36
South Carolina	0.073	48	0.031	8	0.056	41	0.022	10
South Dakota	0.061	44	0.060	47	0.078	47	0.058	48
Tennessee	0.063	45	0.032	12	0.037	20	0.022	12
Texas	0.030	4	0.039	34	0.022	2	0.024	17
Utah	0.029	3	0.034	15	0.052	35	0.036	40
Vermont	0.057	40	0.038	31	0.053	38	0.029	28
Virginia	0.033	7	0.035	22	0.019	1	0.019	4
Washington	0.039	16	0.032	11	0.043	25	0.030	31
West Virginia	0.044	22	0.036	24	0.043	26	0.043	45
Wisconsin	0.036	11	0.029	6	0.046	31	0.019	3
Wyoming	0.051	29	0.073	48	0.046	29	0.045	46

[a]The Regression Volatility measure is the standard deviation in the error term (ε_t) from the regression model specified in equation (3.1) in the text.
[b]The Innovation Volatility measure is the standard deviation in the error term (ε_t) from the time-series model specified in equation (3.2) in the text.

where ln (Income per Capita$_t$) is the natural log of real per capita income in year t. Note that here the procedure estimates one equation for each state, whereas the previous regression method (equation (3.1)) used a panel data set for the 50 states. In equation (3.2), Year$_t$ is a linear time trend variable (from 1969 to 1999), and its slope coefficient, β, estimates the systematic change in income levels over the sample period. This trend-forecasting procedure captures the predictable pattern in state income over time to the extent that the secular pattern is linear. In addition, by detrending the states' fluctuations the forecasting error does not solely represent movements to the upside or downside. For example, suppose income in a state rises consistently. Without detrending, greater fluctuations would reflect net gains in the state's economy. By first taking into account the predictable trends, the residual fluctuations reflect negative as well as positive deviations in a state's economic progress or decline. If income falls short of its expected path, some planned expansions are terminated.

The main parameter of interest in equation (3.2) is ε_t, the regression error term, which captures the difference between the actual and the predicted value of income levels in each year t. These residuals reflect in each year the fluctuation in income level from its long-run trend. The second volatility measure is computed as the standard deviation in ε_t for the 1969–99 period. An increase in the standard deviation of ε_t indicates an increase in volatility.[5] Table 3.2 also presents the values for this second volatility measure for each state under the column labeled "Innovation." The values for both Income per Capita and Income per Worker are listed along with the state rankings based on these values.

Table 3.3 provides a correlation matrix that illustrates the overall degree of similarity among the four measures of state economic volatility. For example, the correlation coefficient between the Regression value and the Innovation value for Income per Capita is 0.72.

TABLE 3.3.   Correlation Matrix for State Volatility Measures

	Regression, Income per Capita	Innovation, Income per Capita	Regression, Income per Worker
Regression, Income per Capita			
Innovation, Income per Capita	0.72		
Regression, Income per Worker	0.72	0.66	
Innovation, Income per Worker	0.64	0.80	0.83

The correlation coefficient between the Regression value and the Innovation value for Income per Worker is 0.83. These simple correlation coefficients indicate that, while the four measures of a state's economic volatility broadly move together, each measure contains unique information. This further suggests that the analyses and conclusions will be somewhat sensitive to which volatility metric one uses.

Figure 3.1 plots the state rankings using the Regression Volatility measure for Income per Capita. By this measure Oklahoma experienced the least volatility (= 0.028) and Alaska experienced the most volatility (= 0.115), more than a fourfold difference. No apparent regional pattern emerges in figure 3.1. The ten most volatile states include four from the South, three from the West, two from the Midwest, and one from the East: Alaska, North Dakota, South Carolina, Nevada, North Carolina, Tennessee, South Dakota, Hawaii, Connecticut, and Arkansas. The ten least volatile states include three from the South, three from the Southwest, two from the Midwest, one from the West, and one from the East: Oklahoma, New Mexico, Utah, Texas, Louisiana, Missouri, Virginia, Ohio, Pennsylvania, and Kentucky. In other words, states from all regions are represented at both the bottom and the top of the volatility scale.

Figure 3.2 plots the state rankings using the volatility measure based on the Innovation index for Income per Capita. Here the most stable state (Missouri = 0.026) and the most volatile state (Alaska = 0.110) differ by a factor of more than four, and the rankings again show geographic diversity. The five least volatile states by this measure are Missouri, Pennsylvania, New Mexico, Ohio, and Colorado, reflecting some overlapping with the prior measure. Alaska, North Dakota, Wyoming, South Dakota, and New Hampshire make up the five most volatile states, which show some consistency with the ranking using the Regression Volatility index.

Figure 3.3 plots the Income per Worker rankings based on the Regression values, and figure 3.4 plots the Income per Worker rankings based on the Innovation values. The per worker rankings depicted in these two figures generally comport with the rankings in the per capita results, although as indicated by the correlation coefficients in table 3.3 each volatility metric yields a unique pattern. Using the Regression index, Virginia exhibits the least volatility, and using the Innovation index Delaware gets the top ranking. Virginia generally ranks among the more stable states by all measures, whereas Delaware fares substantially better under the income per worker measures than it does under the income per capita measures. Two

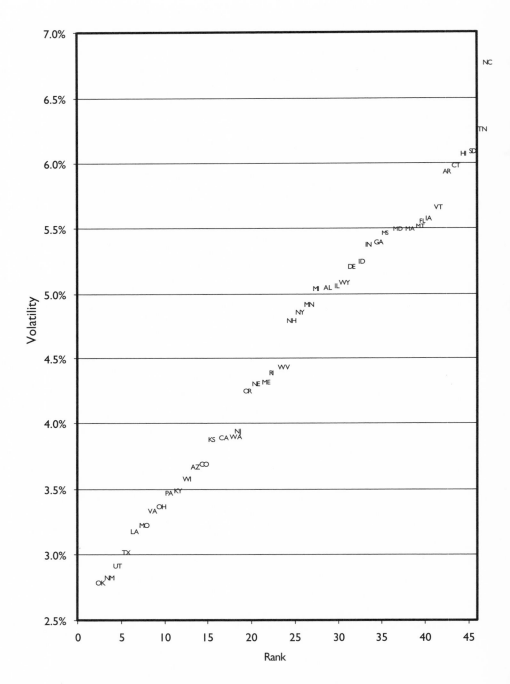

Fig. 3.1. Regression Volatility index, income per capita (values for Nevada, South Carolina, North Dakota, and Alaska exceed the scale)

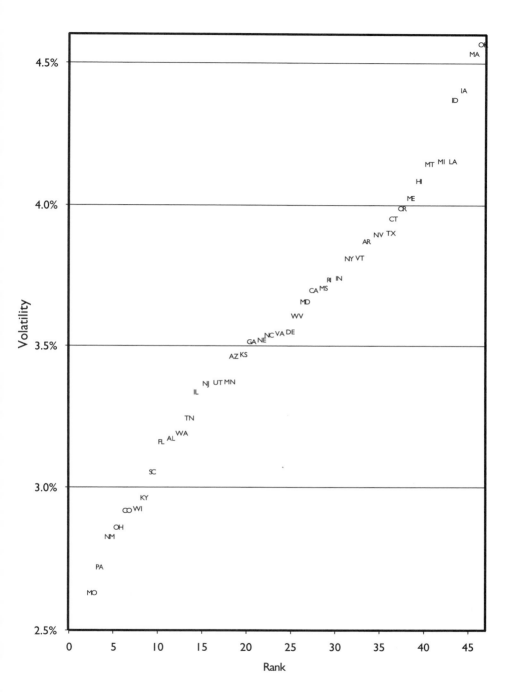

Fig. 3.2. Innovation Volatility index, income per capita (values for New Hampshire, South Dakota, Wyoming, North Dakota, and Alaska exceed the scale)

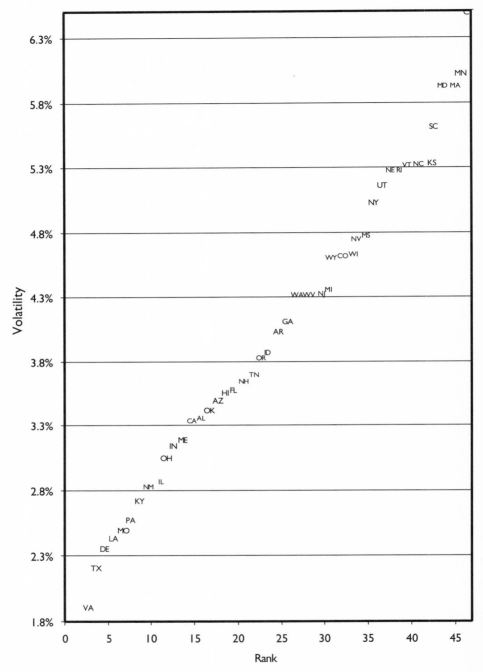

Fig. 3.3. Regression Volatility index, income per worker (volatility values for Iowa, South Dakota, Montana, Alaska, and North Dakota exceed the scale)

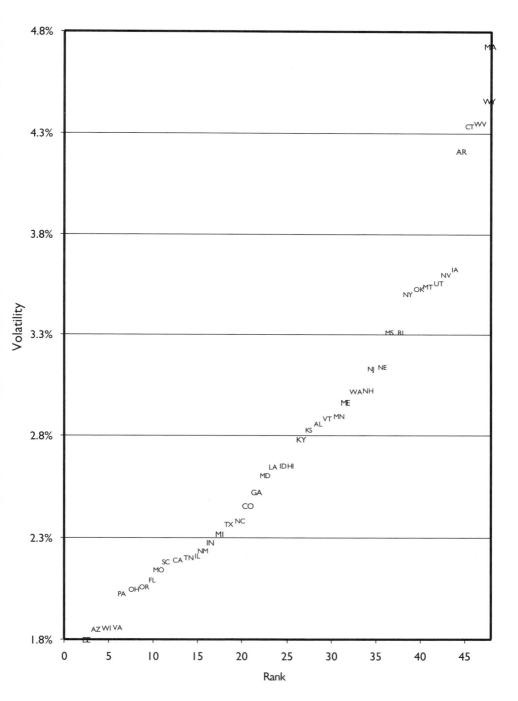

Fig. 3.4. Innovation Volatility index, income per worker (volatility values for South Dakota, Alaska, and North Dakota exceed the scale)

states stand out as the most volatile; Alaska and North Dakota appear by wide margins to be the most volatile states in all four accounts.

Just as the rate of return on an individual stock is more volatile than the return on the stock market as a whole, we would expect the volatility of a single state economy to be greater than the volatility of the U.S. economy as a whole. This simple prediction should hold except in the unlikely event that changes in economic performance are perfectly correlated among the 50 states. To check this thesis and to explore the reasonableness on the volatility indices, the Innovation Volatility index is calculated using aggregate income data for the United States. This procedure estimates the model in equation (3.2) for the comparable time period, 1969–99. For the United States as a whole, the Innovation Volatility index is 0.025 for income per capita and 0.018 for income per worker. Compare these values to those for the individual states in table 3.2. As expected, the U.S. per capita value is less than the value for the least volatile state, Missouri, which has a value of 0.026. Similarly, the U.S. per worker value is less than the value for the least volatile state, Delaware.[6] In other words, the aggregate performance of the U.S. economy by diversifying income among the 50 state economies provides a degree of risk reduction unmatched even by the state with the least volatile economy. As a final and less extreme comparison, consider that the per capita Innovation Volatility for the median state is 0.037, which is nearly 50 percent larger than the volatility for the United States as a whole. The per worker Innovation Volatility for the median state is 0.028, which is over 50 percent larger than the U.S. value.

Why Volatility and the Level of State Income Are Correlated

Macroeconomic theory traditionally treats business-cycle theory and growth theory as unrelated subjects. Implicit in this tradition is the idea that business-cycle volatility and growth are separate phenomena. Only recently, beginning in the 1980s, have economists attempted to draw a causal connection between economic fluctuations and growth. Four theoretical articles suggest that business-cycle volatility will exert a negative impact on an economy's growth path. Bernanke (1983) and Pindyck (1991) argue that, because some investments are irreversible, greater uncertainty about future economic conditions renders firms more reluctant to invest. Increased volatility leads to lower investment, which in turn reduces future output. In a related argument, Aizenman and Marion (1993) suggest that with investment irreversibilities a rise in policy uncertainty reduces investment, an example being so-called capital flight. As an illustration, suppose that a firm constructs a major production facility and policymakers subsequently levy a new tax. Uncertainty about this prospect of course deters the investment in the first place. Ramey and Ramey (1991) argue that if firms must commit to their technology in advance then volatility can lead to lower mean output because firms find themselves producing at suboptimal levels ex post.

Other theoretical models predict a positive relationship between volatility and the level of economic activity. Black (1987) argues that countries may have a choice between high-variance, high-expected returns technologies and low-variance, low-expected returns technologies. In such a world, countries with high average income would also have high variance. Another argument for a positive relationship concerns precautionary savings (Mirman 1971). When faced with greater uncertainty about the future, firms and individuals may increase their savings rates. A precautionary motive for savings implies that higher volatility will lead to a higher savings rate and thereby will result in a higher investment rate. A higher investment rate predictably raises future output rates; this would cause a positive relationship between volatility and income levels.

Note that these theoretical propositions about the impact of volatility apply to the level of economic activity; volatility affects saving and investment behavior that in turn moves an economy to a different point on its long-run growth path. The impact of volatility on economic growth requires additional assumptions, primarily a mechanism whereby changes in investment patterns shift the economy to a new growth path. How volatility changes growth rates requires a more complex model than is required to posit a plausible link between volatility and economic levels.

Despite this critical conceptual caveat the few existing empirical studies have investigated the relationship between volatility and economic growth using U.S. time-series data and cross-country data. Zarnowitz and Moore (1986), studying cyclical behavior in the United States during the twentieth century, find that the standard deviation of GNP growth tends to be higher during periods of lower growth. The study by Zarnowitz and Lambros (1987) finds that an increase in uncertainty about inflation has a short-run negative effect on U.S. GNP growth. Kormendi and McGuire (1985) examine cross-country data and find that higher standard deviations in output growth rates are associated with lower mean growth rates. Grier and Tullock (1989) expand the sample of countries used by Kormendi and McGuire and confirm the negative correlation between volatility and growth. Similarly, Ramey and Ramey (1995) corroborate these two studies using alternative samples of countries, more recent data, and generally a more robust set of conditioning variables. The cross-country study by Aizenman and Marion (1993) also finds a negative relationship between policy uncertainty and income growth rates across countries. Finally, Dawson and Stephenson (1997) find no relationship at the state level between volatility and growth for the period 1970–88.

In summary, on purely theoretical grounds the relationship between volatility and economic performance might be positive or negative, which leaves this issue ripe for empirical exploration. Several studies using U.S. time-series and cross-national data indicate that this relationship is negative. It is important to note that these empirical studies examine the trade-off between volatility and growth rates rather than between volatility and income levels.

State Evidence on the Link between Volatility and State Income

The link between volatility and state income is explored empirically with the model specified in equation (3.3), which augments the model shown in equation (3.1) to include the volatility index, denoted as σ_i:

$$\text{Income per Capita}_{it} = \lambda\sigma_i + \Phi X_{it} + \varepsilon_{it}. \tag{3.3}$$

This specification assumes that σ_i differs across states but not across time for an individual state and that $\varepsilon_{it} \sim N(0, \sigma_i^2)$. Consistent with the analysis in prior chapters, two sets of models are estimated; one reflects income per capita and the other income per worker. In both sets the two alternative measures of σ_i (the volatility measures reported in table 3.2) are used as explanatory variables.

The parameter values in equation (3.3) are estimated using two state samples; one includes all 50 states and the other includes 48 states, dropping Alaska and North Dakota. As the results reported in figure 3.1 indicate, the volatility indices for these two states consistently appear to be statistical outliers. The estimates using the 50-state sample are provided in table 3.A2 in the appendix at the end of this chapter, and the estimates using the 48-state sample are shown in table 3.4.[7] The first two columns denominate the dependent variables in terms of income per capita, and the last two columns denominate the dependent variable in terms of income per worker. Equation (3.3) is again estimated as a panel model using the feasible generalized least squares iterative technique. As described for equation

(3.1), the model corrects for heteroskedasticity across states and estimates a state-specific coefficient of the AR(1) process.

The main finding of interest in table 3.4 concerns the estimated coefficients on the volatility variables. In all four models the coefficient is positive and significant at either the 1 or the 5 percent level. Put simply, high-income states experience higher volatility than low-income states.[8] Regarding the magnitude of the relationship, first consider the effect of a one standard deviation increase in the Regression Volatility index for income per capita. That is, what is the predicted impact on state per capita income if volatility increases by one standard deviation (which equals 0.012 in the 48-state sample)? Using the estimated coefficient shown in table 3.4 (= 2.981) this implies a 3.44 percent increase in income per capita, or about $762 per capita evaluated at the sample mean value (= 0.0344 × $22,148). Using the results for the Innovation Volatility index, a one standard deviation

TABLE 3.4.   Relationship between Level and Volatility of Income, 1969–99 (48-state sample, excluding Alaska and North Dakota)

Independent Variables	Dependent Variable = Income per Capita[a]		Dependent Variable = Income per Worker[a]	
	Income Volatility Based on Regression Residuals[b]	Income Volatility Based on Innovation Residuals[c]	Income Volatility Based on Regression Residuals[b]	Income Volatility Based on Innovation Residuals[c]
Income Volatility (per Capita	2.981	3.748	0.523	2.066
or per Worker)	(7.48)**	(6.68)**	(1.96)*	(3.85)**
Education (% of population,	0.026	0.025	0.009	0.010
BA or higher)[d]	(29.26)**	(26.90)**	(12.58)**	(13.35)**
ln (Population)	0.006	0.012	0.013	0.015
	(1.03)	(1.80)	(2.81)**	(3.24)**
Urban Population (% of	0.002	0.003	0.003	0.003
population)[d]	(9.34)**	(9.71)**	(15.51)**	(15.37)**
Population Age 18 to 64	0.014	0.015	0.006	0.006
(% of population)[d]	(8.82)**	(9.40)**	(5.64)**	(4.90)**
Constant	8.334	8.159	9.673	9.612
	(75.5)**	(63.0)**	(112.4)**	(105.6)**
Wald chi-squared	3363**	3038**	1385**	1335**
Total panel observations	1,488	1,488	1,488	1,488

Note: z-statistics are shown in parentheses.

[a]Entered as natural logarithmic transformations, denominated in real (2000) dollars.

[b]Income Volatility is measured as the standard deviation in the regression residuals from the core model referenced in table 3.1.

[c]Income Volatility is measured as the standard deviation in the regression residuals from the time-series model referenced in equation (3.2).

[d]Variables denominated as fractions are multiplied by 100 in the estimation models.

* Indicates significance at the 5 percent level for a two-tailed test. ** Indicates significance at the 1 percent level for a two-tailed test.

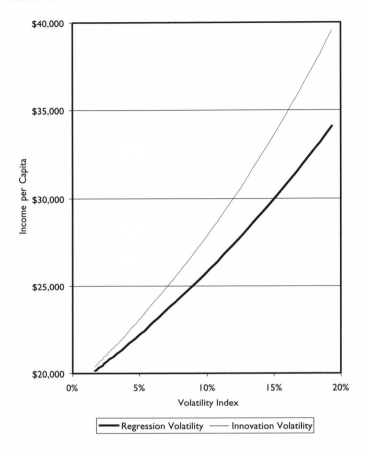

Fig. 3.5.   Estimated trade-off between volatility and income per capita

increase corresponds to a 3.04 percent increase in income per capita, or about $674 per capita evaluated at the sample mean. A similar comparative static calculation using the Income per Worker estimates implies that a one standard deviation increase in volatility is correlated with a 0.72 percent increase ($306 per worker) based on the Regression Volatility index and a 1.77 percent increase ($748 per worker) based on the Innovation Volatility index.

These estimated correlations between volatility and state income are displayed graphically in figure 3.5 (for income per capita) and figure 3.6 (for income per worker). The lines trace out the predicted values for income for alternative volatility levels based on the estimated coefficients shown in table 3.4. The predicted values for in-

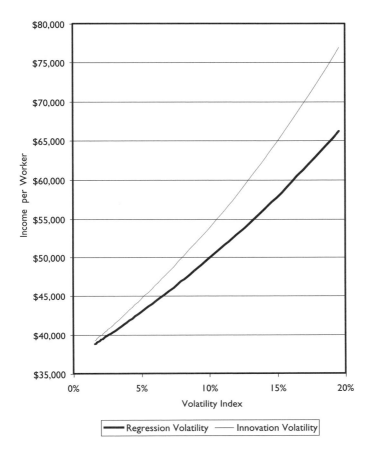

Fig. 3.6.   Estimated trade-off between volatility and income per worker

come hold the other factors in the model (e.g., education level, state size, and so forth) constant at their mean values. The lines in figures 3.5 and 3.6 are nonlinear because the predicted income values are converted back into levels rather than graphed in log form.[9]

Commentary

This chapter elevates the importance of the volatility of state economies, a neglected aspect in the evaluation of state economic performance. Just as modern financial theory judges asset values based on a mean-variance criterion, a two-dimensional analysis of economy performance seems appropriate. The four volatility indices developed in the chapter indicate considerable differences among states in volatility, which lends credence to the importance of this dimension of economic performance. The analysis reveals a systematic, positive relationship between state volatility and state income, akin to the positive relationship between the risk and rate of return on financial assets. Relatively high levels of state income appear to reflect a risk premium to compensate at least in part for relatively high degrees of income volatility. In this perspective, the volatility in state income weakens a worker's enthusiasm to relocate into that state, and this deterrent to labor market adjustments would push up a state's income per worker. A state with relatively low volatility may appeal to the risk preferences of some workers and may overshadow the attraction of potentially higher incomes available in other states.

Subsequent chapters explore the stability of state fiscal conditions and its link to state economic performance. Economic volatility translates into fiscal volatility for the obvious reason that personal income, retail sales, and corporate profits largely determine the tax base that supports state revenues.

Appendix

TABLE 3.A1. Summary Statistics and Data Sources[a]

Variable	Mean	Median	Standard Deviation
Income per Capita[b,c]	$22,148	$21,770	$4,450
Income per Worker[b,c]	$42,302	$41,368	$5,582
Volatility in Income per Capita — Regression method[b]	0.047	0.049	0.012
Volatility in Income per Capita — Innovation method[b]	0.038	0.037	0.008
Volatility in Income per Worker — Regression method[b]	0.043	0.043	0.014
Volatility in Income per Worker — Innovation method[b]	0.029	0.027	0.009
Education (% of population, BS or higher)[c]	17.2	16.8	5.2
Population[c,d]	4,888,045	3,350,522	5,098,383
Urban Population (% of population)[c]	64.7	67.6	21.9
Population Age 18 to 64 (% of population)[c]	59.7	60.1	2.8

[a]Summary statistics for 1969–99 period for the 48-state sample, excluding Alaska and North Dakota.

[b]Denominated in real (2000) dollars. Data from U.S. Bureau of the Census Web Site. The Income per Capita and Income per Worker variables are entered into the regression models as natural log transformations. The nonlogged summary statistics are reported here.

[c]Data from U.S. Bureau of the Census Web Site.

[d]The Population variable is entered into the regression models as a natural log transformation. The nonlogged summary statistics are reported here.

TABLE 3.A2. Relationship between Level and Volatility of Income, 1969–99
(50-state sample)

Independent Variables	Dependent Variable = Income per Capita[a]		Dependent Variable = Income per Worker[a]	
	Income Volatility Based on Regression Residuals[b]	Income Volatility Based on Innovation Residuals[c]	Income Volatility Based on Regression Residuals[b]	Income Volatility Based on Innovation Residuals[c]
Income Volatility (per Capita or per Worker)	2.602	2.280	0.472	1.217
	(7.33)**	(4.48)**	(1.87)	(2.54)**
Education (% of population, BA or higher)[d]	0.025	0.026	0.008	0.009
	(28.92)**	(27.19)**	(11.73)**	(12.41)**
ln (Population)	0.003	0.007	0.007	0.010
	(0.61)	(1.01)	(1.44)	(1.97)*
Urban Population (% of population)[d]	0.002	0.003	0.003	0.003
	(9.59)**	(9.72)**	(15.02)**	(14.82)**
Population Age 18 to 64 (% of population)[d]	0.015	0.015	0.008	0.007
	(9.43)**	(9.67)**	(6.39)**	(5.93)**
Constant	8.335	8.281	9.693	9.657
	(75.8)**	(66.2)**	(109.8)**	(108.7)**
Wald chi-squared	3405**	3133**	1325**	1314**
Total panel observations	1,550	1,550	1,550	1,550

Note: z-statistics are shown in parentheses.

[a]Entered as natural logarithmic transformations, denominated in real (2000) dollars.

[b]Income Volatility is measured as the standard deviation in the regression residuals from the core model references in table 3.1.

[c]Income Volatility is measured as the standard deviation in the regression residuals from the time-series model referenced in equation (3.2).

[d]Variables denominated as fractions are multiplied by 100 in the estimation models.

* Indicates significance at the 5 percent level for a two-tailed test. ** Indicates significance at the 1 percent level for a two-tailed test.

Chapter 4

Demise of the State Sales Tax

At the dawn of the twenty-first century slightly more than one-third of all economic activity in the United States passed through the public sector. In round numbers, the federal, state, and local governments collected about $3.5 trillion in revenues out of a $10 trillion U.S. economy. The federal government collected just more than one-half of these revenues, state governments collected slightly more than one-fourth, and local governments took in slightly more than one-fifth.

The relative sizes of the public and private sectors in the United States remained fairly stable for much of the second half of the twentieth century. This is certainly the case when compared to the pre–World War II period. As a benchmark for comparison, in 1900 the public sector accounted for less than 7 percent of the economic activity in the United States. Similarly, and again by long-run historical standards, the relative sizes of the federal, state, and local governments during the postwar period remained fairly stable.[1]

Beneath these signs of post–World War II stability a revolution occurred in state fiscal policy, particularly with respect to the structure of state taxes.

State Revenue Sources

Funds to finance the activities of American state governments come from three principal sources: tax revenues (43 percent), intergovernmental revenues (22 percent), and insurance trust revenues (20 percent). Regarding tax revenues states rely largely on three instruments: general and selective sales taxes, individual (or personal) income taxes, and corporation net income taxes. These three instruments generate about 90 percent of state tax revenues. In addition, state lawmakers have direct statutory authority to determine these three revenue sources. For these reasons, revenue policy deliberations in America's state capitols center most often on the appropriate level and mix of the sales tax, the individual income tax, and the corporation income tax.

This chapter focuses on these three major tax instruments, first examining the variation among states and the evolution of state tax structures over time. It then provides new measures of marginal tax rates and the progressivity or regressivity of sales and individual income taxes for each state. These critical indicators of the state tax burden lay the groundwork for the analysis in chapter 5 of the impact of alternative tax instruments on state economic performance.

The Composition of State Tax Revenues

In the late twentieth century, a remarkable change occurred in the composition of state tax revenues. In 1969 sales taxes reigned as the instrument of choice, accounting for almost 80 percent of tax revenues in the median state. In that year, in the median state sales tax revenues exceeded individual income tax revenues by a factor of 4 and exceeded corporation income tax revenues by a factor of 11. This overwhelming dominance of sales tax revenues fell dramatically in the three decades that followed (see fig. 4.1).[2]

In 1998 (the most recently available data) sales tax revenues remained the largest tax revenue source, although its share of total tax revenues declined to 53 percent in the median state, down from its 80 percent share just 30 years earlier. Near the end of the century, sales tax revenues exceeded personal income tax revenues only by a factor of 1.3 and exceeded corporation net income taxes by a factor of 8 in the median state. A simple linear projection of these revenue composition trends indicates that by about 2004 states will rely almost evenly on sales taxes and personal income taxes (about 46 percent each), with only a slight decline in the corporation income tax as a revenue source (projected to remain at about 8 percent). The linear trend line projections indicate that by about 2005 state individual income tax revenues will exceed sales tax revenues and by 2010 will comprise 50 percent of all state tax revenues.

Table 4.1 shows the composition of taxes for the individual states. This table shows the share of all tax revenues raised from the three major tax instruments in 1998 and how much these shares changed between 1969 and 1998. Consistent with the general trends already described, in 1969 individual income tax revenues exceeded sales tax revenues in only 5 states; by 1998 income tax revenues exceeded sales tax revenues in 12 states, or in almost 25 percent of the states. Between 1969 and 1998 individual income tax revenues as a share of total taxes increased in 84 percent of the states and the median increase was 18 percentage points. Sales tax revenues as a share of total tax revenues

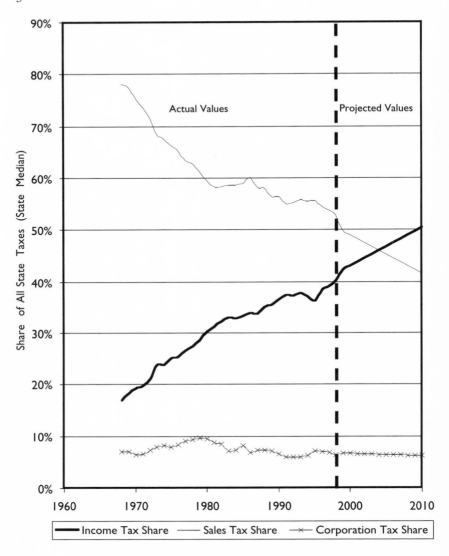

Fig. 4.1.   Changing composition of state tax revenues

fell in 88 percent of the states; the median decrease was 16 percentage points. Corporation income tax revenues as a share of total tax revenues decreased in 58 percent of the states, but the median decrease was minor, less than 1 percentage point.

These data reveal, in the aggregate and at the individual state

TABLE 4.1. Major Sources of State Tax Revenues: 1998 and Changes since 1969

	Personal Income Tax		Sales Tax		Corporation Income Tax	
	Share in 1998 (%)	Change since 1969	Share in 1998 (%)	Change since 1969	Share in 1998 (%)	Change since 1969
Alabama	36	21	59	−20	5	−1
Alaska	0	−53	30	−8	70	61
Arizona	29	13	63	−15	8	3
Arkansas	37	23	56	−22	7	−1
California	46	22	44	−19	9	−4
Colorado	53	23	42	−19	5	−4
Connecticut	39	39	55	−27	6	−13
Delaware	62	8	21	−12	17	3
Florida	0	0	93	−7	7	7
Georgia	48	30	45	−27	7	−3
Hawaii	35	5	63	−2	2	−3
Idaho	42	11	52	−10	6	−2
Illinois	39	39	50	−50	11	11
Indiana	43	20	47	−29	10	9
Iowa	43	21	52	−21	5	0
Kansas	41	19	52	−20	7	1
Kentucky	40	22	54	−20	6	−1
Louisiana	29	19	64	−18	7	−1
Maine	42	42	53	−47	5	5
Maryland	50	8	46	−6	5	−3
Massachusetts	58	18	32	−11	10	−7
Michigan	35	14	52	−15	13	1
Minnesota	46	7	47	−4	7	−3
Mississippi	22	16	72	−13	6	−3
Missouri	45	25	50	−27	5	2
Montana	56	18	34	−18	10	0
Nebraska	40	21	54	−24	6	2
Nevada	0	0	100	0	0	0
New Hampshire	8	3	63	−32	30	30
New Jersey	39	37	53	−27	8	−10
New Mexico	27	15	67	−19	6	3
New York	54	7	37	−3	9	−4
North Carolina	48	20	45	−15	8	−5
North Dakota	20	3	70	−10	9	7
Ohio	43	43	52	−48	5	5
Oklahoma	46	31	49	−30	5	−1
Oregon	78	17	15	−12	6	−5
Pennsylvania	35	35	56	−29	9	−6
Rhode Island	43	43	53	−31	4	−12
South Carolina	40	20	56	−15	4	−5
South Dakota	0	0	95	−5	5	5
Tennessee	3	0	87	2	10	−2
Texas	0	0	100	0	0	0
Utah	41	12	53	−11	6	−1
Vermont	44	3	51	−2	5	−1
Virginia	55	22	40	−18	5	−4
Washington	0	0	100	0	0	0
West Virginia	33	23	59	−30	8	7
Wisconsin	49	−2	44	6	7	−4
Wyoming	0	0	100	0	0	0

Note: Share in 1998 measures the percentage of all state tax revenues raised from that tax instrument. The shares for the three tax instruments may not sum to 100 because of rounding.

Change since 1969 measures the change in the percentage raised from that tax instrument since 1969. For example, in Alabama the personal income tax share of all tax revenues increased 21 percentage points between 1969 and 1998.

level, the distinct structural shift in the composition of state tax revenues during the last three decades of the twentieth century. The personal income tax steadily replaced the sales tax.[3]

Convergence and Divergence in State Tax Policies

A related question is whether tax policies have become more uniform among the American states over time. The variation across states in tax composition and its temporal evolution is used to address this question. The coefficient of variation in the share of revenue raised from each of the three major tax revenue sources over the period 1969–98 is shown in figure 4.2.[4]

A pattern of convergence among states appears with regard to their reliance on the individual income tax, with the fall in the coefficient of variation particularly steep in the early 1970s. The coefficient of variation for the corporation income tax share also drops in the early 1970s, indicating initial convergence. The period from 1978 through 1983 shows sharp divergence, followed by a pattern that resembles a random walk, which continued through the 1990s. That is, no clear pattern of convergence or divergence exists for the corporation income tax. The diversity among states in reliance on corporation income tax revenues in 1998 was almost exactly the same as it was in 1981.

A noteworthy development illustrated in figure 4.2 is that beginning in 1978 and continuing throughout the 1990s the dispersion in corporation income tax revenues among states exceeded the dispersion in income tax revenues. The coefficient of variation for the sales tax series rises noticeably from 1969 until 1982, indicating divergence in this tax instrument. After 1982 the dispersion in sales tax revenues remains virtually unchanged through 1998.

As an additional check on the convergence or divergence of taxes among states figure 4.3 displays the coefficient of variation in the average tax rates for individual income taxes, sales taxes, and total state taxes.[5] These data reveal once again an almost continuous convergence among states in the average tax rates for the individual income tax. However, for sales taxes the average tax rates among states diverge slightly over these three decades, with the main increase occurring between 1969 and 1982, which corroborates the pattern in the sales taxes shown in figure 4.2. The dispersion pattern in the average tax rate for total state taxes remains virtually unchanged throughout the three decades, indicating no tendency toward tax policy convergence.

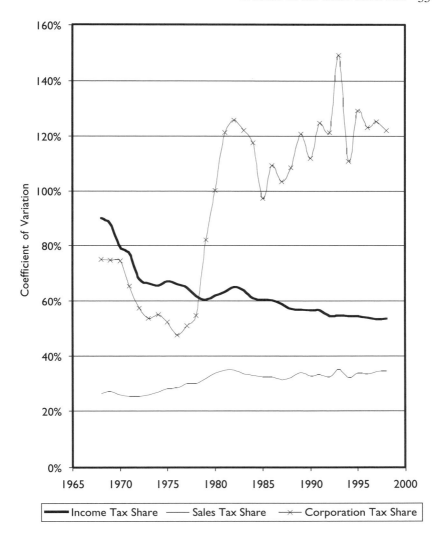

Fig. 4.2.   Convergence/divergence among states in the structure of taxes (measured by tax instrument's share of total taxes)

In sum, these findings indicate that while reliance on the individual income tax increased in almost all states (42 out of 50) the increases were larger in the low income tax states relative to the high income tax states. The combined effect of these adjustments created more uniformity among states with respect to revenues from the individual

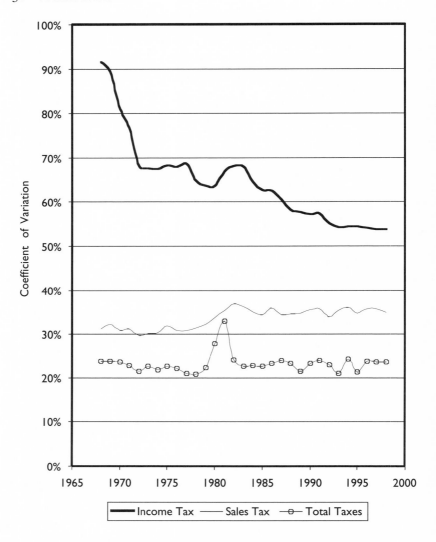

Fig. 4.3. Convergence/divergence among states in average tax rates

income tax. The average tax rate on individual income likewise tended toward greater uniformity between 1969 and 1998. In contrast, while almost all states (44 out of 50) reduced their reliance on sales tax revenues, the decreases occurred in high and low sales tax states alike. In other words, states with heavy reliance on sales tax revenues and those with light reliance cut back in about equal proportions. As a result, diversity among states in the average tax rate for sales taxes slightly increased over the period. In 1998 states exhibited broader diversity with respect to corporation income taxes than personal income taxes, a notable evolution in state fiscal structures, as shown in figure 4.2.

Estimates of State Marginal Tax Rates

The analysis expands prior studies of state taxes first by estimating the marginal tax rate and the average tax rate for sales taxes and individual income taxes in each state. Past studies have estimated marginal and average rates only for total state and local taxes. The separate estimates for sales and income taxes facilitate comparisons within and across states in the relative degree of progressivity or regressivity of these two predominant state tax instruments. These estimates of sales and income marginal tax rates are used to examine the effects of fiscal policy on state economic performance in chapter 5. As discussed there in additional detail, marginal and average tax rates are required for an appropriate specification of the statistical analysis.

Koester and Kormendi (1989) developed a procedure to estimate marginal tax rates that was subsequently employed by Mullen and Williams (1994) and Besci (1996). Koester and Kormendi estimated these rates for a cross-section of 63 countries using the aggregate of all country tax revenues. Mullen and Williams and Besci estimated these rates for the American states, but, as noted, both studies use total state and local tax revenues. The novelty here is to estimate the marginal and average rates separately for state sales taxes and state individual income taxes. For comparison, the analysis also estimates the marginal and average rates for total state taxes.

The Koester-Kormendi procedure to estimate the marginal tax rate uses the model shown in equation (4.1):[6]

$$\text{Revenue}_t = \lambda + \text{MTR} \times \text{Income}_t + \varepsilon_t, \tag{4.1}$$

where the subscripts refer to year t and the estimation uses the sample period 1969 to 1998 (the most recently available data). For comparison, the time period in the Mullen and Williams (1994) study began in 1969 and ended in 1986, and the time period in the Besci (1996) study began in 1961 and ended in 1992. Revenue_t is a state's revenue from the specific tax being analyzed (either sales taxes, individual income taxes, or total taxes) in year t. Income_t is a state's total personal income in year t. In this specification $\text{MTR} \times \text{Income}_t$ measures revenues that respond to income changes and the coefficient on income, MTR, gives the effect on revenues of a small change in income in period *t*. In other words, the regression coefficient on Income$_t$ (denoted MTR) estimates the marginal tax rate (by definition, the change in revenue in response to a change in income).[7] Under the Koester-Kormendi procedure the estimated MTR does not apply to any one individual; rather, it approximates the marginal tax rate for the representative (average) individual in the state. The constant term in the regression equation, λ, proxies tax revenues that are not affected by changes in income and, it is important to note, would not be expected to influence individual incentives with respect to changes in income.[8]

Three final details about the estimation procedure require explanation. First, each of the estimation models includes a first-order autoregressive term to correct for serial correlation in the error terms (denoted ε_t in equation (4.1)). Second, certain states are excluded from the regression analysis.[9] Third, the estimates of the marginal tax rates in six states use a slightly modified sample period. These six states experienced major structural changes in their tax codes in the early 1970s.[10]

The estimated tax rates for each state are reported in table 4.2 (for the personal income tax), table 4.3 (for the sales tax), and table 4.4 (for total state taxes). Before discussing the state-specific results for marginal tax rates, the procedure for estimating average tax rates is described.

Estimates of State Average Tax Rates

The commonly used procedure to estimate average tax rates (ATR) is shown in equation (4.2):[11]

$$\text{ATR}_t = \frac{\text{Revenue}_t}{\text{Income}_t}, \qquad (4.2)$$

where the subscripts again refer to year *t*. As defined in equation (4.1) Revenue$_t$ is a state's revenue from the specific tax being analyzed (either sales taxes, personal income taxes, or total taxes) in year *t* and Income$_t$ is a state's total personal income in year *t*. Finally, the estimates of the average tax rates for each state are computed as the mean value of ATR$_t$ for the 1969–98 period.[12]

State-Specific Results for Marginal Rates and Average Rates

Table 4.2 presents the estimated marginal and average rates for the personal income tax and the rank in these rates among the 50 states.

TABLE 4.2. State Personal Income Taxes: Marginal and Average Tax Rates, 1969–98

	Marginal Rate (%)	Rank	Average Rate (%)	Rank
Alabama	1.96	17	1.40	19
Alaska		1		1
Arizona	1.75	14	1.35	18
Arkansas	2.61	31	1.67	26
California	2.82	36	2.08	36
Colorado	2.44	24	1.79	30
Connecticut		1		1
Delaware	3.22	43	3.26	49
Florida		1		1
Georgia	2.70	33	1.93	32
Hawaii	3.36	45	2.83	44
Idaho	2.97	41	2.19	40
Illinois	1.94	16	1.47	20
Indiana	2.92	40	1.66	25
Iowa	2.90	38	2.12	37
Kansas	2.50	25	1.58	24
Kentucky	2.90	39	1.86	31
Louisiana	1.52	12	0.85	11
Maine	3.26	44	1.75	28
Maryland	2.60	30	2.36	42
Massachusetts	3.92	49	3.04	45
Michigan	2.54	27	1.99	34
Minnesota	3.49	47	3.11	46
Mississippi	1.60	13	1.05	13
Missouri	2.42	22	1.50	22
Montana	2.39	21	2.00	35
Nebraska	2.43	23	1.47	21
Nevada		1		1
New Hampshire		1		1
New Jersey	2.28	19	1.13	15
New Mexico	2.18	18	1.10	14
New York	3.49	48	3.14	48
North Carolina	3.19	42	2.41	43
North Dakota	1.17	11	1.01	12
Ohio	2.80	35	1.29	16
Oklahoma	2.59	29	1.53	23
Oregon	4.10	50	3.28	50
Pennsylvania	1.85	15	1.33	17
Rhode Island	2.62	32	1.76	29
South Carolina	2.52	26	1.97	33
South Dakota		1		1
Tennessee		1		1
Texas		1		1
Utah	2.89	37	2.16	39
Vermont	2.37	20	2.24	41
Virginia	2.73	34	2.15	38
Washington		1		1
West Virginia	2.55	28	1.68	27
Wisconsin	3.46	46	3.14	47
Wyoming		1		1

Note: A rank of 1 indicates the state with the lowest tax rate; a rank of 50 indicates the highest tax rate. The ten states without an income tax on earned income receive a rank of 1, and the next lowest rate receives a rank of 11.

TABLE 4.3. State Sales Taxes: Marginal and Average Tax Rates, 1969–98

	Marginal Rate (%)	Rank	Average Rate (%)	Rank
Alabama	2.90	20	3.69	36
Alaska	0.56	5	0.93	5
Arizona	3.80	40	3.98	43
Arkansas	3.92	41	3.85	39
California	2.82	16	2.90	17
Colorado	1.89	6	2.35	8
Connecticut	3.60	34	3.59	33
Delaware		1		1
Florida	4.28	44	4.02	44
Georgia	2.52	13	3.18	24
Hawaii	6.19	50	5.69	50
Idaho	3.69	37	3.23	25
Illinois	2.46	11	2.90	15
Indiana	2.86	18	3.34	27
Iowa	3.32	30	3.01	19
Kansas	3.16	27	2.90	16
Kentucky	3.63	35	3.71	37
Louisiana	2.91	21	3.35	28
Maine	3.50	32	3.98	42
Maryland	2.41	10	2.62	10
Massachusetts	2.13	8	2.23	6
Michigan	3.11	26	2.96	18
Minnesota	3.71	38	3.30	26
Mississippi	4.87	46	5.14	48
Missouri	2.72	14	2.70	11
Montana		1		1
Nebraska	3.17	28	3.01	20
Nevada	5.49	48	5.09	45
New Hampshire		1		1
New Jersey	3.10	25	2.80	13
New Mexico	5.36	47	5.14	47
New York	2.16	9	2.42	9
North Carolina	2.90	19	3.11	22
North Dakota	4.36	45	3.67	35
Ohio	2.92	22	2.82	14
Oklahoma	2.85	17	2.78	12
Oregon		1		1
Pennsylvania	2.79	15	3.08	21
Rhode Island	3.05	24	3.42	30
South Carolina	3.27	29	3.92	41
South Dakota	3.56	33	3.82	38
Tennessee	4.04	42	3.88	40
Texas	4.15	43	3.52	32
Utah	3.63	36	3.61	34
Vermont	3.03	23	3.36	29
Virginia	1.97	7	2.34	7
Washington	5.67	49	5.49	49
West Virginia	3.71	39	5.09	46
Wisconsin	3.40	31	3.13	23
Wyoming	2.49	12	3.45	31

Note: A rank of 1 indicates the state with the lowest tax rate; a rank of 50 indicates the highest tax rate. The 4 states without a general sales tax receive a rank of 1, and the next lowest rate receives a rank of 5.

TABLE 4.4.   Total State Taxes: Marginal and Average Tax Rates, 1969–98

	Marginal Rate (%)	Rank	Average Rate (%)	Rank
Alabama	5.12	14	5.40	27
Alaska	2.35	2	4.42	9
Arizona	6.01	28	5.70	32
Arkansas	6.93	43	5.97	36
California	6.32	33	5.74	33
Colorado	4.50	7	4.41	8
Connecticut	6.71	39	5.06	21
Delaware	5.32	17	5.31	26
Florida	4.57	9	4.28	6
Georgia	5.59	20	5.57	30
Hawaii	9.76	50	8.84	50
Idaho	7.15	46	5.87	35
Illinois	4.92	12	4.76	17
Indiana	6.46	34	5.30	25
Iowa	6.55	35	5.48	28
Kansas	6.09	30	4.95	19
Kentucky	6.92	42	6.05	39
Louisiana	4.79	10	4.67	15
Maine	7.09	44	6.06	40
Maryland	5.23	16	5.27	24
Massachusetts	6.67	38	6.05	38
Michigan	6.66	37	5.80	34
Minnesota	7.68	48	7.04	48
Mississippi	6.91	40	6.57	45
Missouri	5.43	18	4.45	12
Montana	4.30	6	4.01	5
Nebraska	5.93	26	4.76	16
Nevada	5.49	19	5.09	22
New Hampshire	2.31	1	2.39	1
New Jersey	5.88	24	4.45	10
New Mexico	7.98	49	6.60	46
New York	6.13	32	6.20	43
North Carolina	6.62	36	6.10	42
North Dakota	6.11	31	5.15	23
Ohio	5.95	27	4.41	7
Oklahoma	5.69	22	4.60	14
Oregon	5.20	15	4.56	13
Pennsylvania	5.07	13	5.05	20
Rhode Island	5.88	25	5.66	31
South Carolina	6.03	29	6.34	44
South Dakota	3.87	4	3.96	4
Tennessee	4.54	8	4.45	11
Texas	4.15	5	3.52	3
Utah	6.91	41	6.10	41
Vermont	5.70	23	5.99	37
Virginia	4.91	11	4.80	18
Washington	5.67	21	5.49	29
West Virginia	7.15	45	7.16	49
Wisconsin	7.33	47	6.84	47
Wyoming	2.49	3	3.45	2

Note: A rank of 1 indicates the state with the lowest tax rate; a rank of 50 indicates the highest tax rate.

The 7 states without an individual income tax and the 3 states without taxes on earned income receive a rank of 1. North Dakota, which has the lowest marginal income tax rate among states that tax earned income, receives a rank of 11, and so on. The state with the highest marginal income tax rate, Oregon, receives a rank of 50.

The rates reported in table 4.2 reveal that state personal income taxes are overwhelmingly progressive, a finding consistent with conventional wisdom. In 39 of the 40 states with a personal income tax on earned income, the estimated marginal tax rate exceeds the average tax rate. The sole exception is Delaware, where the average rate barely exceeds the marginal rate, indicating a slightly regressive structure. Incidentally, Delaware does not have a general sales tax; instead it relies heavily on the corporation income tax and on corporate chartering fees for state revenues. Oregon, which also levies no sales tax, exhibits the highest marginal tax rates on personal income, followed by Massachusetts, New York, Minnesota, and Wisconsin.

Table 4.3 shows the estimated average and marginal rates for the sales tax. Again the table shows the ranking for the rates among states. Here the four states without a general sales tax receive a rank of 1. The state (that has a general sales tax) with the lowest sales tax rate (Alaska) receives a rank of 5, and so on. The state with the highest sales tax rate (Hawaii) receives a rank of 50.

Table 4.3 reveals an important and unconventional finding with respect to state sales taxes: this tax is progressive in a surprisingly large number of states. Of the 46 states with a general sales tax, the marginal tax rate exceeds the average tax rate in 22 of them. In essence, almost half of the states have a progressive sales tax. Conventional wisdom holds that the sales tax is regressive, whereas the income tax tends to be progressive. However, some states do exempt from the general sales tax basic necessities such as food and prescription and nonprescription drugs. Other states apply a differentially lower tax rate to necessities. An increasing number of states have instituted "sales tax holidays," or special shopping periods during which no sales taxes are levied. Such exemptions and special rates would make the sales tax relatively more progressive.

Table 4.4 presents the average and marginal rates and the state rankings for state total taxes. Based on total taxes, 40 out of the 50 states exhibit a marginal tax rate in excess of the average tax rate. This estimate of the degree of overall tax progressivity approximates the results reported by Mullen and Williams (1994) and Besci (1996) using all state and local taxes. Regarding the individual state rankings for total taxes, New Hampshire shows the lowest marginal rates, followed by Alaska, Wyoming, South Dakota, and Texas. At the other end of the spectrum, the highest marginal tax rates are seen in Hawaii, New Mexico, Minnesota, Wisconsin, and Idaho.

Commentary

The displacement of the sales tax by the individual income tax stands out as a fundamental transformation in state fiscal structures in the 1970s, 1980s, and 1990s. In the late 1990s the sales tax remained the largest tax revenue source for state governments, yet this paled in comparison to the dominance of the sales tax three decades earlier. In almost every state the income tax encroached on the sales tax as a revenue source. In 1998, almost one in four states raised more revenues from personal income taxes than from sales taxes, up from about one in ten in 1969. The share of state revenues raised from the corporation net income tax remained steady throughout the 1970s, 1980s, and 1990s, and the linear trend projection indicates this tax instrument will continue to account for about 8 percent of tax revenues in the typical state. Linear projections of the historical trends indicate that state income tax revenues will soon reach parity with sales tax revenues in the typical state. By 2010, the typical state will raise half of its tax revenues from the individual income tax.

The sharp evolution toward greater uniformity with regard to the individual income tax represents a second fundamental development in state fiscal policy. In contrast, we observe a trend toward greater diversity among states with regard to sales taxes. It is important to note that the data reveal no overall fiscal convergence among states based on total state taxes.

The estimates for total state taxes indicate that the marginal rate exceeds the average rate in 40 of the 50 states, evidence of broad-based progressivity in the overall structure of state taxes. For the personal income tax, the marginal rate exceeds the average rate in all but one state. The finding that sales taxes appear to be progressive in about half of the states is quite surprising. Chapter 5 explores the consequences of these facts about state tax structures on state economic performance.

Chapter 5

Economic Consequences of State Tax Policy

The effect of state fiscal policy in boosting or restraining economic performance remains an unsettled question, despite its obvious relevance to policymakers. The existing empirical research provides surprisingly little clarity. Chapter 1 described the persistent growth rate differentials among states in the 1970s, 1980s, and 1990s. The absence of long-run, "automatic" economic convergence depicted in chapter 2 suggests that state policies may exert an important influence on the relative performance of state economies. At least conceptually, it is hard to think of an influence on economic activity that would be more direct than taxes. Yet, the sizable number of empirical studies offers a host of conflicting results concerning the degree to which taxes affect state economic performance.[1] The conflicting results in large part stem from technical difficulties inherent in the empirical estimation problem.

Three studies provided critical breakthroughs in the empirical research program: Koester and Kormindi (1989), Mullen and Williams (1994), and Besci (1996). The latest of these studies, by Besci, incorporates and expands upon the two earlier studies, and the analysis that follows adopts the Besci methodology with a few new wrinkles. The Besci method corrects several problems in the methods employed in prior articles that estimated the impact of taxes on state economies. First, prior studies used proxies for the average tax rate as independent variables in state growth regressions. In contrast, economic theory stresses that marginal tax rates influence behavior and ultimately the factors that determine aggregate economic performance.[2] Besci follows Koester and Kormindi and Mullen and Williams in using marginal tax rates in the empirical specifications.

The second innovation in the Besci method is to control for the degree of progressivity of state tax policy and thereby isolate the distortionary effects of changes in marginal tax rates. This control technique relates to the way a state government balances its budget in response to a change in the marginal tax rate. The way a government's budget is balanced (e.g., by raising or lowering taxes generally and raising or lowering spending) may have independent effects on a state's economy. The effect of changes in other fiscal policies potentially biases the estimates of tax effects unless the empirical model properly controls for such influences. As an example, suppose a state raises its personal income tax rate and in turn tax revenues rise. The uses to which these new revenues are put may convey economic consequences. Funding additional infrastructure investments, education, public safety programs, or public welfare programs may have different effects on the state's economy, independent of the consequences associated with the change in the income tax per se. Alternatively, the state's fiscal response might be to cut some other tax, thereby leaving total revenues and total spending unchanged. This framework for analysis is commonly referred to as a revenue-neutral change in taxes. The Besci technique adopted here provides a method to control for possible differences in the economic impact from these sorts of secondary, or indirect, responses to tax changes.[3] In effect, it examines the impact on state economies from a revenue-neutral change in the marginal tax rate.

The third desirable feature in the Besci method is its focus on the relative economic performance of American states.[4] Examining each state's economic performance relative to other states does two things analytically. First, it filters out the impact of global and national economic conditions, as well as the impact of national fiscal and monetary policies that influence all state economies. Second, it takes into account the competitive nature of state governments, in contrast to an encompassing national government that has considerable monopoly power in setting tax rates. Taking the competitiveness of state governments into account is particularly important in analyzing and comparing the effects of specific types of taxes. For example, suppose the federal government imposes a national consumption (sales) tax. This might reduce consumption, increase national savings, and redirect resources into growth-enhancing capital investment activities. However, the impact of a sales tax at a subnational (state) level may be quite different. Rather than redirecting resources from consumption to investment activities, a state sales tax may simply encourage the location or migration of productive factors or it may encourage consumers to cross state boundaries to make purchases. The potential influence of factor and consumer mobility illustrates the importance of using a state's relative tax rate in the analysis. Suppose a state leaves its tax rate unchanged while another state implements a tax cut. Firms, workers, and consumers may benefit from relocating into the tax-cutting state, affecting both states' economies, even though taxes in one state remained the same. Using a measure of relative taxes seeks to capture the impact of the interdependency of tax policies among states.

In summary, the Besci (1996) estimation procedure contains several features that lend precision to the analysis employed in this chapter. These include (1) using the correct measure of taxes (the marginal tax rates as derived in chap. 4), (2) controlling for the influence of how other fiscal policies adjust to tax changes, and (3) using measures of relative tax rates. The analysis performed here extends prior studies (including Besci's) by isolating and comparing the separate effects of state sales taxes and state income taxes.

Specification Issues, Variable Definitions, and Data Sample

Equation (5.1) shows the Besci specification.

$$\text{State Income}_i = a + b\,(\text{MTR}_i) + c\,(\text{Regressivity Index}_i) + \varepsilon_i, \tag{5.1}$$

where the subscript i denotes the value of a variable in state i and

State Income$_i$ = real income per capita in state i (or real income per worker as indicated) averaged over the 1969–98 period,

MTR$_i$ = the marginal tax rate in state i (estimated using the procedure described in chap. 4 and shown in tables 4.2 and 4.3),

Regressivity Index$_i$ = the average tax rate in state i (estimated using the procedure described in chap. 4) divided by the marginal tax rate in state i, and

ε_i = a random disturbance term.

The main models of interest contain separate variables (measuring the MTR and the Regressivity Index) for the sales tax and the personal income tax. For comparison, results are also reported for models that examine total state taxes and therefore use aggregate measures of the MTR and the Regressivity Index. These aggregate models using total state taxes correspond to the specification used by Besci.

The values for each of the variables are entered into the regression models as log differences from the average (median) state values for the reasons previously discussed. This means that the results show the effects of relative tax rates on relative income levels (or relative income growth rates).[5] All variables reflect values for the period 1969 through 1998.

A final methodological detail concerns the samples used to estimate equation (5.1). Here and in most of the subsequent analyses of state fiscal policies I follow the conventional practice of omitting three states: Alaska, Hawaii, and Wyoming. The fiscal experiences of these states represent clear statistical outliers. Data values with large deviations from the average sample values usually exert undue influence in statistical estimation and thereby result in biased parameter estimates. The source of the large deviations in Alaska and Wyoming stems from their unusually heavy reliance on energy severance taxes. In Hawaii, the state government funds all public education expenditures. All other states delegate to local governments the responsibility for funding education for grades K–12. For comparison, however, table 5.1A in the appendix at the end of this chapter reports the results for a sample that includes all 50 states. In the models that include separate variables for the sales tax and the personal income tax, the 14 states that do not levy one or both of these types of taxes are excluded. In these 14 states the marginal and average tax rates are zero for at least one of the required variables, and the Regressivity Index is therefore undefined.

Results: Marginal Tax Rates and State Income

The results of estimating equation (5.1) are shown in tables 5.1 and 5.2. Table 5.1 reports the impact of marginal tax rates on income per capita and income per worker. Table 5.2 reports the impact on income growth rates.

Regarding sales taxes, the findings indicate that higher marginal rates have a negative and statistically significant impact on state income levels and growth rates. Consider first the effect on per capita income reported in Model 1 of table 5.1. The estimated coefficient on the marginal tax rate for the sales tax is −0.51. This coefficient indicates that a marginal sales tax rate that is 1 percent above the national average reduces per capita income by 0.51 percent below the median level of per capita income.

To illustrate the magnitude of this effect suppose Kansas, the state that happens to have the median marginal sales tax rate, increased its sales tax rate by 10 percent. This would amount to a change in the marginal rate from 3.2 percent to 3.5 percent. The regression results indicate that per capita income in Kansas would fall by 5.1 percent (= 0.1 × −0.51) relative to the median per capita income for all states. Using the median value for state income in 1999 (which equals $27,812 in 2000 dollars), the 10 percent tax hike would predictably reduce real per capita income in Kansas by $1,408. Of course, the model parameters apply equally to a sales tax reduction; a 10 percent cut in the sales tax would predictably stimulate economic activity and eventually add $1,408 to per capita income in Kansas.

The impact on income per worker is shown in Model 3 in table 5.1. There the estimated coefficient on the marginal tax rate for the sales tax is −0.31. Continuing with the Kansas example, the predicted ef-

TABLE 5.1. Impact of Marginal Tax Rates on State Income, 1969–98[a]

Independent Variables	Dependent Variable = Income per Capita		Dependent Variable = Income per Worker	
	Model 1	Model 2	Model 3	Model 4
Marginal Tax Rate: Sales Tax	−0.51	—	−0.31	—
	(−6.43)**		(−3.10)**	
Marginal Tax Rate: Personal Income Tax	0.01	—	−0.01	—
	(0.17)		(−0.17)	
Marginal Tax Rate: Total Taxes[b]	—	−0.15	—	−0.05
		(−1.90)		(−0.84)
Sales Tax Regressivity	−0.56	—	−0.20	—
	(−4.02)**		(−0.98)	
Income Tax Regressivity	0.04	—	−0.04	—
	(0.17)		(−0.35)	
Total Tax Regressivity[b]	—	−0.30	—	−0.14
		(−1.20)		(−0.57)
Constant	−0.02	−0.02	−0.00	0.00
	(−1.78)	(−1.09)	(−0.16)	(0.22)
R-squared	0.64	0.06	0.27	0.01
F-statistic	18.9**	1.87	3.41*	0.37
Number of observations	36[c,d]	47[c]	36[c,d]	47[c]

Note: t-statistics are shown in parentheses.

[a]These regressions measure the dependent and independent variables as log differences from their national averages, as reflected by the values in the median state.

[b]Total Taxes include state taxes on individual income, sales, and corporation net income.

[c]Alaska, Hawaii, and Wyoming are omitted.

[d]Sample omits states that do not have a general sales tax or an individual income tax on earned income.

* Indicates significance at the 5 percent level for a two-tailed test. ** Indicates significance at the 1 percent level for a two-tailed test.

fect of a 10 percent increase in the marginal sales tax rate would be a decline in income per worker equal to $1,375.[6]

Table 5.2 reports the models that examine the impact of taxes on state growth rates. Two models are reported corresponding to the two methods for computing per capita income growth rates, the continuously compounded method (Model 1) and the least squares method (Model 2). In both growth models the estimated coefficients on the marginal tax rate for the sales tax are statistically significant at the 0.01 confidence level. In Model 1 the projected impact of a 10 percent marginal tax rate increase (relative to the median tax rate) is to shave 0.08 percentage points off a state's annual growth rate. As a benchmark, this would reduce real annual growth in the median state from 1.69 percent to 1.61 percent. In Model 2 the projected impact is a 0.06 percentage point drop in annual growth.

In short, the empirical models bring to light substantial economic

TABLE 5.2.   Impact of Marginal Tax Rates on State Income Growth, 1969–98[a]

Independent Variables	Dependent Variable = Continuously Compounded Growth Rate	Dependent Variable = Least Squares Growth Rate
	Model 1	Model 2
Marginal Tax Rate: Sales Tax	−0.46	−0.37
	(−4.79)**	(−2.80)**
Marginal Tax Rate: Personal Income Tax	0.01	0.20
	(0.14)	(1.77)
Sales Tax Regressivity	−0.13	0.39
	(−0.63)	(1.04)
Income Tax Regressivity	0.07	−0.04
	(0.45)	(−0.20)
Initial State Income per Capita	−0.83	−0.50
	(−4.68)**	(−2.00)*
Constant	−0.02	−0.02
	(−1.03)	(−0.67)
R-squared	0.60	0.43
F-statistic	8.98**	7.77**
Number of observations[b]	36	36

Note: t-statistics are shown in parentheses.

[a]These regressions measure the dependent and independent variables as log differences from their national averages, as reflected by the values in the median state.

[b]Sample omits Alaska, Hawaii, Wyoming, and states that do not have a general sales tax or an individual income tax on earned income.

* Indicates significance at the 5 percent level for a two-tailed test. ** Indicates significance at the 1 percent level for a two-tailed test.

consequences of state sales taxes. The same cannot be said about personal income taxes. Somewhat surprisingly, the analysis finds no evidence of a systematic effect of the state personal income tax on the level or growth rate in state income. None of the estimated coefficients on the marginal income tax rate is significant at conventional levels in any of the models reported in tables 5.1 and 5.2. Finally, regarding the aggregate, total tax variables, the effect of the marginal tax rate is consistently negative, but these coefficients fail to meet conventional levels of statistical confidence.

Commentary

Two important studies in the 1990s—Mullen and Williams 1994 and Besci 1996—find significant effects of state and local taxes on the relative performance of state economies. These pathbreaking studies provide considerable guidance for the appropriate specification of estimation models. This chapter extends these newly developed techniques to examine separately the impact of state sales taxes and individual income taxes. Two findings stand out from the empirical analysis of the last three decades of the twentieth century. First, marginal tax rates matter for sales taxes but not for individual income taxes. Second, states suffer a substantial penalty for levying a marginal sales tax rate that is high in relation to other states. Of course, the reverse also applies. Substantial economic benefits redound to states with relatively low marginal sales tax rates.

Appendix: Why State Sales Taxes Matter and State Income Taxes Do Not

Economic theory provides useful models to anticipate markets' reactions to taxes. However, the actual effects of taxes depend crucially on individual behavior, and therefore theory alone provides only a guide to the range of possible outcomes. The standard theoretical analysis of the individual income tax provides a classic illustration. The theory posits two offsetting behavioral incentives. First, the personal income tax discourages the incentive to work because the opportunity cost of leisure (or any nonwork activity) is reduced. When after-tax pay declines, less income is foregone by choosing leisure activities over work time. Offsetting this effect, if leisure is a "normal good," a reduction in after-tax income reduces the demand for leisure and nonwork activities. Whether (and to what extent) an income tax increases or decreases hours worked thus depends upon which of these two effects dominates. Theory provides no unambiguous prediction about the net effect on the labor market. Rather, empirical analysis is required to get at the actual impact of income taxes on labor market adjustments. Thus, the finding that economic activity in the states appears unaffected by relative marginal income taxes is not a rejection of the theory.

The observed adverse impact of state sales taxes on state economic activity also squares with basic theory. In this case, standard theory provides two perspectives that yield equivalent outcomes. One perspective treats the sales tax as an increase in the cost of production, which thereby shifts upward the supply function. The other treats the sales tax as a reduction in the revenues retained by sellers, which thereby shifts downward the firm's after-tax revenue function. That is, after-tax revenues diverge from the market demand function that reflects the prices consumers are willing to pay.

In either perspective the predicted result of levying a sales tax is to increase market prices and reduce output, except in special and improbable cases.[7] Intuitively, the impact of the sales tax is analogous to a general, broad-based increase in the cost of production. The shortcoming in the pure theory of the sales tax lies in its inability to predict the magnitude of its effects on prices and output. These depend upon the relevant demand and supply elasticities. For example, if consumers are highly price sensitive, the imposition of a sales tax results in large reductions in consumption and output, with most of the tax burden falling on producers and employees. In relatively price-inelastic markets, the consumption and output effects are less severe and most of the tax burden is passed through to consumers in the form of price increases.

A recent empirical analysis by Besley and Rosen (1999) of price data for specific commodities and sales tax rates in different U.S. cities sheds considerable light on this issue.[8] Besley and Rosen examine the extent to which commodity prices across cities are affected by sales taxes, controlling for other factors (such as costs) that also affect prices. For some commodities (Big Macs, eggs, Kleenex, Monopoly games, and spin balances), the after-tax price increases by just the amount of the sales tax, a result consistent with the standard competitive model that assumes a perfectly elastic supply. However, for other commodities (bananas, bread, Crisco, milk, shampoo, soda, and boys underwear), the after-tax price appears to overshift; prices rise by more than the sales tax. For example, raising a dime in sales tax revenue per unit sold increases the price per unit by more than a dime, and in some cases by more than 20 cents. Tax overshifting may be the result of imperfectly competitive market structures. If prices for commodities go up more than on a one-for-one basis, as the Besley-Rosen results indicate, then sales taxes are more burdensome than the usual analyses would suggest. These findings by Besley and Rosen provide evidence at the microeconomic level to account for the results in chapter 5 on the aggregate impact of sales taxes on state economies.

TABLE 5.A1.   Impact of Marginal Tax Rates on State Incomes, 1969–98 (50-state sample)[a]

Independent Variables	Dependent Variables = Income per Capita		Dependent Variables = Income per Worker	
	Model 1	Model 2	Model 3	Model 4
Marginal Tax Rate: Sales Tax	−0.34	—	−0.22	—
	(−2.56)**		(−2.34)**	
Marginal Tax Rate: Personal Income Tax	0.09	—	0.03	—
	(1.24)		(0.48)	
Marginal Tax Rate: Total Taxes[b]	—	−0.10	—	−0.03
		(−1.13)		(−0.56)
Sales Tax Regressivity	−0.49	—	−0.16	—
	(−3.24)**		(−0.85)	
Income Tax Regressivity	0.12	—	0.00	—
	(1.10)		(0.03)	
Total Tax Regressivity[b]	—	0.02	—	0.03
		(0.12)		(0.17)
Constant	−0.01	−0.01	0.01	0.01
	(−0.37)	(−0.37)	(0.35)	(0.57)
R-squared	0.46	0.05	0.21	0.01
F-statistics	15.36**	1.23	2.49	0.39
Number of observations	37[c]	50	37[c]	50

Note: t-statistics are shown in parentheses.

[a]These regressions measure the dependent and independent variables as log differences from their national averages, as reflected by the values in the median state.

[b]Total Taxes include state taxes on individual income, sales, and corporation net income.

[c]Sample omits states that do not have a general sales tax or an individual income tax.

* Indicates significance at the 5 percent level for a two-tailed test. ** Indicates significance at the 1 percent level for a two-tailed test.

Chapter 6

Reliability of Revenues from Alternative Tax Instruments

More than 200 years ago Adam Smith maintained that reliability is one of the most important attributes of a good tax system. Economists have since formalized this concept into a basic principle of public finance, and most policymakers quickly discover its verity through practical experience.[1] Governments benefit from a reliable revenue stream for the obvious reason that spending commitments must be made before revenues are actually in hand. When revenues fall short of budgetary commitments, elected officials find themselves in a politically precarious position. They face a limited set of possible fiscal policy responses, and none is pleasant: renege on spending commitments, raise taxes, print money, issue debt, or some combination of the four. In years when actual revenues exceed budgetary commitments, elected officials sometimes respond gleefully; yet a revenue windfall that results in an unanticipated budget surplus is not costless. Policy options were forgone or at least delayed. Some desired programs went unfunded for the fiscal year, or an opportunity to enact a tax cut was missed or delayed. In the event of either a revenue shortfall or a windfall, policymakers face inferior policy options relative to those that are available when actual revenues meet budgetary expectations.[2]

Various constraints limit the options available to policymakers in the American states to deal with revenue shortfalls, and these make the predictability of revenue flows particularly important. Foremost among these, the U.S. Constitution prohibits American state governments from raising public revenue through money creation. In addition, a mix of state constitutional provisions, statutory budget rules, and a competitive bond market constrains the ability of states to issue debt in response to revenue shortfalls. Given these constraints, American state governments for the most part achieve fiscal balance through adjustments in spending and taxes.

The need to adjust taxes in response to cyclical revenue fluctuations distorts resource mobilization and thereby creates a source of inefficiency that impairs economic activity. This follows because the deadweight cost (or excess burden) of taxation depends on the square of the tax rate. Classic works in public finance such as those by Barro (1979), Kydland and Prescott (1980), and Lucas and Stokey (1983) use this standard proposition to formalize the tax-smoothing thesis as a way to minimize the excess burden of taxation over the business cycle. This thesis, in brief, argues that to promote economic development governments should shun cyclical changes in taxes. Constraints on the use of debt financing by state governments to achieve tax smoothing mean that the reliability of revenue flows represents a crucial factor in the evaluation of alternative tax instruments.[3]

This chapter analyzes the reliability of state revenues from sales taxes and individual income taxes, the two largest sources of state tax revenues, as discussed in detail in chapter 4. The initial task is to construct an indicator of revenue volatility, which of course reflects the opposite of revenue reliability. This metric is then used to compare the volatility of sales tax revenues and individual income tax revenues for each state. Finally, the analysis examines the related issue of tax structure diversification and its impact on revenue volatility in the states.

The Measurement of Tax Revenue Volatility

The first order of business is to compute a relevant measure of tax revenue volatility. Generally the procedure entails estimating the revenue volatility for each tax type (sales and individual income), given the existing tax structure in a state, and then standardizing this volatility measure by its share of total revenues raised. The basic measure of revenue volatility is the standard deviation of the deviation in revenue from its long-run trend line.[4]

The deviation in revenue from its long-run trend is estimated with the following regression equation:

$$\ln (\text{Tax Revenue}_t / \text{Income}_t) = \alpha + \beta(\text{Year}_t) + \varepsilon_t, \tag{6.1}$$

where $\ln (\text{Tax Revenue}_t / \text{Income}_t)$ is the natural log of revenue from a specific tax instrument (here, the sales tax or the individual income tax) as a share of state personal income in year t. This specification of the dependent variable thus measures tax revenue fluctuations in relation to a state's economic fluctuations. In other words, state economic conditions naturally influence state tax revenues, but here the analysis seeks to focus on how much more (or less) revenues fluctuate compared to the state's economy. Year_t is a linear time trend variable (from 1968 to 1998). Its coefficient, labeled β in equation (6.1), estimates the systematic growth or decline in tax revenue as a share of income over the three-decade sample period. This detrending procedure removes the predictable, secular patterns from the revenue variables.[5] The main parameter of interest, ε_t (the regression error term), measures the difference between the actual and the predicted value of tax revenue as a share of income in each year t. This reflects the unanticipated component of tax revenue in each year.[6]

The second step in the measurement procedure computes the standard deviation in ε_t for the 1968–98 period. The standard deviation denotes the volatility in the unanticipated revenue component, and an increase in the standard deviation of ε_t indicates an increase in the volatility of tax revenue relative to state income.

A valid comparison between the volatility of the sales tax and the income tax requires a final transformation of these standard deviations. An example illustrates. Suppose on average sales taxes generate $1 billion in state revenues and income taxes generate $3 billion. In that case, the standard deviation in sales tax revenues (say, $100 million, or 10 percent) will be less than the standard deviation in income tax revenues (say, $300 million, again 10 percent) simply because sales taxes raise less revenue than income taxes. The relevant comparison therefore needs to project volatility (the standard deviation) under the assumption that both taxes generate equal revenues. To make this apples-to-apples comparison, the standard deviations are transformed under the assumption that each tax alone raised revenues equal to the combined amount. Returning to the numerical example, the standard deviations in sales tax revenues and income tax revenues are projected assuming that each generated $4 billion instead of $1 billion and $3 billion.[7]

Table 6.1 presents the revenue volatility measures for each state for individual income taxes and sales taxes. For the reasons previously stressed, direct comparisons across states are not valid without making further adjustments for differences in the total revenues generated by the specific taxes. However, the procedure does allow within-state comparisons of the relative volatility in these two tax instruments. The middle columns provide the revenue-equivalent volatility measures for the individual income tax and the sales tax. The last column of table 6.1 denotes whether the sales tax or the income tax produces a less volatile revenue stream. Among the states that levy both types of taxes, 62 percent (23 out of 37 states) experience less volatility in individual income tax revenues than in sales tax

TABLE 6.1. Volatility in Revenues from Sales Taxes and Individual Income Taxes, 1968–98

	Sales Tax	Income Tax	Tax with Less Volatility
Alabama	0.0025	0.0022	Income
Alaska			
Arizona	0.0041	0.0036	Income
Arkansas	0.0047	0.0025	Income
California	0.0030	0.0037	Sales
Colorado	0.0029	0.0029	Income
Connecticut			
Delaware			
Florida			
Georgia	0.0043	0.0028	Income
Hawaii	0.0038	0.0056	Sales
Idaho	0.0049	0.0038	Income
Illinois	0.0027	0.0020	Income
Indiana	0.0059	0.0038	Income
Iowa	0.0053	0.0052	Income
Kansas	0.0049	0.0027	Income
Kentucky	0.0067	0.0031	Income
Louisiana	0.0042	0.0053	Sales
Maine	0.0054	0.0052	Income
Maryland	0.0033	0.0019	Income
Massachusetts	0.0047	0.0036	Income
Michigan	0.0068	0.0073	Sales
Minnesota	0.0036	0.0067	Sales
Mississippi	0.0055	0.0058	Sales
Missouri	0.0035	0.0027	Income
Montana			
Nebraska	0.0030	0.0037	Sales
Nevada			
New Hampshire			
New Jersey	0.0041	0.0057	Sales
New Mexico	0.0047	0.0157	Sales
New York	0.0057	0.0040	Income
North Carolina	0.0057	0.0020	Income
North Dakota	0.0054	0.0115	Sales
Ohio	0.0027	0.0037	Sales
Oklahoma	0.0062	0.0021	Income
Oregon			
Pennsylvania	0.0028	0.0061	Sales
Rhode Island	0.0034	0.0027	Income
South Carolina	0.0036	0.0042	Sales
South Dakota			
Tennessee			
Texas			
Utah	0.0036	0.0040	Sales
Vermont	0.0074	0.0044	Income
Virginia	0.0040	0.0013	Income
Washington			
West Virginia	0.0049	0.0048	Income
Wisconsin	0.0058	0.0037	Income
Wyoming			

Note: Sales taxes include revenues from the general sales tax and selective sales taxes. Income taxes include revenues from individual income taxes. Income tax volatility measures are not computed for states without a tax on earned income (e.g., wages and salaries). Sales tax volatility measures are not computed for states without a general sales tax. See chapter 4 for a complete discussion of the specific tax structures in each state.

revenues.[8] In the other 14 states that levy both types of taxes, sales tax revenues exhibit less volatility than income tax revenues.

The finding that the volatility in sales tax revenues exceeds the volatility in income tax revenues in almost two-thirds of the states (for which a direct comparison is possible) generally runs counter to the conventional wisdom in public finance. This conventional wisdom goes roughly as follows: sales tax receipts vary less than income tax receipts because individuals' consumption expenditures vary less than their incomes. The logic behind this thinking traces to Milton Friedman's classic formulation of the permanent (or life cycle) income hypothesis. In that framework a family's anticipated lifetime income determines its consumption patterns more than its income in any single period. In essence, families smooth their consumption patterns over time. This implies that families spend a higher share of their annual income in earlier (low-income) years and a smaller share of annual income in later (high-income) years. For example, if family income rises or falls by 10 percent in a given year, consumption would rise or fall by less than 10 percent. For this reason, sales tax revenues tied to consumption spending are widely believed to be less volatile than revenues based on annual incomes. However, the results reported in table 6.1 suggest that this intuitively appealing theoretical framework inaccurately characterizes the state experiences in the last 30 years of the twentieth century.

The Influence of Tax Diversification on Revenue Volatility

A closely related fiscal policy issue concerns how the diversification of tax instruments affects revenue volatility. Is the revenue stream from multiple tax instruments less volatile than the revenue stream from a single tax instrument? The main lesson from modern portfolio theory suggests that diversification provides a critical mechanism to reduce risk. When asset values fluctuate over time, an investor may potentially increase the value of his or her portfolio by holding multiple assets instead of a single asset. This holds so long as the fluctuations in asset values are not perfectly correlated. By analogy, so long as the fluctuations in the tax revenues from two tax instruments are not perfectly correlated, the potential exists for a state to reduce volatility by levying multiple tax instruments.

This question is addressed by comparing the volatility in the combined revenues from sales and income taxes to the volatility if the state were to rely on a single tax instrument to raise the equivalent revenue. To make this comparison, the analysis focuses on the tax instrument that exhibits the lower volatility (as denoted in table 6.1). Table 6.2 reports the results of the tax diversification analysis.

Consider the results for Alabama as an illustration of these findings. In Alabama individual income tax revenues are less volatile than sales tax revenues (based on the revenue-equivalent analysis described for table 6.1). The income tax accounts for 37 percent of the combined revenues from the income and sales taxes (based on the tax structure in Alabama in 1998). The third column of table 6.2 shows the volatility in the combined revenues from the sales tax and the individual income tax, which is 0.0014 for Alabama. Note that the volatility of combined tax revenues is computed using the same procedure described earlier, that is, the standard deviation in the deviations from the 30-year trend. The fourth column shows the projected volatility in income tax revenues if it were used as the sole tax instrument (= 0.0022). That is, instead of its actual mix of income taxes (37 percent of combined revenues) and sales taxes (63 percent of combined revenues), suppose Alabama relied solely upon the income tax to generate the amount of revenue generated by the two taxes combined. The projected volatility of income tax revenues thus assumes its revenue share increased from 37 percent to 100 percent. Under that scenario, the projected standard deviation in income tax revenues is 0.0022.[9] Finally, the last column in table 6.2 reports the percentage difference between the projected revenue volatility under the single tax instrument and the volatility under the existing multitax structure. In Alabama, this projection indicates that volatility would be increased by 34 percent if it relied exclusively on the income tax as compared to its diversified tax structure. In effect, this result suggests that tax revenue diversification in Alabama reduces revenue volatility relative to an exclusive reliance on the income tax.

In general, a positive value in the last column of table 6.2 indicates that using a single tax instrument would increase revenue volatility relative to a diversified tax structure that includes both income and sales taxes. A negative value in the last column indicates that using a single tax revenue source would reduce volatility compared to the actual multitax mix of sales and income taxes. In other words, in that case the volatility in one tax source is so great that it offsets any potential benefits from tax diversification. Overall, the analysis finds that in 35 percent of the states (13 out of 37) the projected revenue volatility would be less under a single tax source than under the status quo mix of income and sales taxes. In 7 of these states (Kansas, Kentucky,

TABLE 6.2. Revenue Volatility from Tax Diversification versus a Single Tax Instrument, 1968–98

	Tax with Less Volatility	Less Volatile Tax as a Share of Income and Sales Taxes (in %)	Income Tax Plus Sales Tax: Standard Deviation	Projected Standard Deviation If State Relied Solely on the Less Volatile Tax	Projected % Change in Volatility If State Relied Solely on the Less Volatile Tax
Alabama	Income	37	0.0014	0.0022	34
Arizona	Income	32	0.0033	0.0036	8
Arkansas	Income	40	0.0023	0.0025	8
California	Sales	49	0.0019	0.0030	37
Colorado	Income	55	0.0026	0.0029	9
Georgia	Income	52	0.0015	0.0028	48
Hawaii	Sales	64	0.0038	0.0038	−0.5
Idaho	Income	45	0.0032	0.0038	16
Illinois	Income	43	0.0019	0.0020	7
Indiana	Income	48	0.0031	0.0038	19
Iowa	Income	45	0.0023	0.0052	56
Kansas	Income	44	0.0029	0.0027	−7
Kentucky	Income	43	0.0046	0.0031	−48
Louisiana	Sales	69	0.0040	0.0042	5
Maine	Income	44	0.0030	0.0052	42
Maryland	Income	52	0.0022	0.0019	−13
Massachusetts	Income	65	0.0035	0.0036	4
Michigan	Sales	60	0.0039	0.0068	42
Minnesota	Sales	51	0.0042	0.0036	−18
Mississippi	Sales	77	0.0051	0.0055	7
Missouri	Income	47	0.0027	0.0027	1
Nebraska	Sales	57	0.0027	0.0030	8
New Jersey	Sales	58	0.0032	0.0041	21
New Mexico	Sales	71	0.0067	0.0047	−43
New York	Income	60	0.0034	0.0040	15
North Carolina	Income	52	0.0022	0.0020	−11
North Dakota	Sales	77	0.0057	0.0054	−6
Ohio	Sales	54	0.0029	0.0027	−9
Oklahoma	Income	48	0.0031	0.0021	−51
Pennsylvania	Sales	62	0.0028	0.0028	−0.3
Rhode Island	Income	45	0.0018	0.0027	31
South Carolina	Sales	58	0.0026	0.0036	28
Utah	Sales	56	0.0028	0.0036	24
Vermont	Income	46	0.0052	0.0044	−17
Virginia	Income	58	0.0018	0.0013	−36
West Virginia	Income	36	0.0043	0.0048	10
Wisconsin	Income	52	0.0035	0.0037	4

Note: The following states are omitted because they do not levy both types of taxes: Alaska, Connecticut, Delaware, Florida, Montana, Nevada, New Hampshire, Oregon, South Dakota, Tennessee, Texas, Washington, and Wyoming.

Maryland, North Carolina, Oklahoma, Vermont, and Virginia) exclusive reliance on the income tax would reduce revenue volatility. In the other 6 states (Hawaii, Minnesota, New Mexico, North Dakota, Ohio, and Pennsylvania) exclusive reliance on the sales tax would reduce revenue volatility relative to the status quo tax mix.

In summary, the findings indicate that in nearly two-thirds of the states, tax diversification effectively reduces revenue volatility, as standard portfolio theory would predict. In one-third of the states, relying on a single-tax instrument would predictably reduce revenue volatility relative to the status quo level of tax diversification.

It is important to note that this analysis evaluates the existing tax diversification against an extreme alternative, relying exclusively on a single tax instrument. It does not necessarily follow that the states have selected an optimal mix of sales and income taxes from the perspective of minimizing revenue volatility. Put differently, could a state further reduce its revenue uncertainty by selecting an alternative mix of tax instruments? As a rough indicator, note that in 16 of the 37 states (43 percent) analyzed in table 6.2, the tax source that exhibited less volatility accounted for less than 50 percent of the combined sales and income tax revenues. In all but 1 of these states (the exception is California) the income tax shows less volatility yet raises less revenue than the sales tax. This provides at least a preliminary indication that further substitution of income taxes for sales taxes could reduce overall revenue volatility in these states.

Commentary

The conventional wisdom that sales taxes generate a more reliable revenue stream than income taxes does not square with the observed fiscal experiences in nearly 2 out of 3 American states. The analysis in this chapter discovers that income tax revenues are less volatile than sales tax revenues in 23 of the 37 states that levy both types of taxes. The analysis also finds that in two-thirds of the states, tax diversification reduces revenue volatility relative to a tax structure that relies exclusively on a single tax instrument. However, the comparison of the tax composition with the sources of volatility identifies at least 16 states that could likely reduce revenue volatility by altering their current mix of tax instruments. In 15 of these states, the projections indicate that increased reliance on income taxes and less reliance on sales taxes would likely result in an overall improvement in revenue stability.

Of course reliability is only one attribute of a good tax system, and other forces surely come into play in the choice of fiscal instruments. However, the desire for a tax structure that enhances revenue stability, in conjunction with the negative consequences of sales taxes on economic performance, offers two powerful explanations for the pervasive shift in state governments away from sales taxes and toward increased reliance on income taxes. In light of these findings the demise of state sales taxes represents a rational response by state policymakers to the negative attributes of this tax instrument.

Chapter 7

State Budgets Outgrow State Incomes

The size of state governments increased between 1969 and 1998, a fact not likely to surprise even the most casual follower of public affairs. Less well known perhaps is the extent to which programs funded by state governments expanded during these three decades. Government spending in the typical (median) state grew from $1,696 per capita in 1969 to $3,593 in 1998 (both numbers are denominated in constant 2000 dollars). Figure 7.1 illustrates this growth, which amounts to a 75 percent (continuously compounded) real increase, or an average annual growth rate of 2.6 percent. By comparison, personal income per capita in the median state grew by 49 percent in inflation-adjusted dollars, an average annual growth rate of 1.7 percent. Over these three decades, state governments annually grew nearly 1 percentage point faster than state income.[1]

Figure 7.2 illustrates the growth of state governments in a slightly different way, in this case using the ratio of government spending to income in the median state. In 1969, state spending equaled 10.7 percent of state income. This climbed to 13.3 percent in 1998, a 21 percent increase.[2] Again, this alternative indicator reveals that state government spending annually grew almost 1 percentage point faster than income in the typical state. In short, during the last three decades of the twentieth century the size of the state public sector expanded markedly in relation to the private sector. This spending surge surely resulted in part from the progressive nature of state tax structures. As we found in chapter 4, the state personal income tax was progressive in 39 out of 40 states and the state sales tax was progressive in 22 out of 46 states. Tax progressivity ensures that government revenue growth will outpace income growth even without an explicit tax rate increase.

What happened to the size of the federal government during this period of state government expansion? The path of federal expenditures as a share of U.S. income, as shown in figure 7.2, tracks the path of state expenditures between 1969 and the mid-1980s. In 1969 fed-

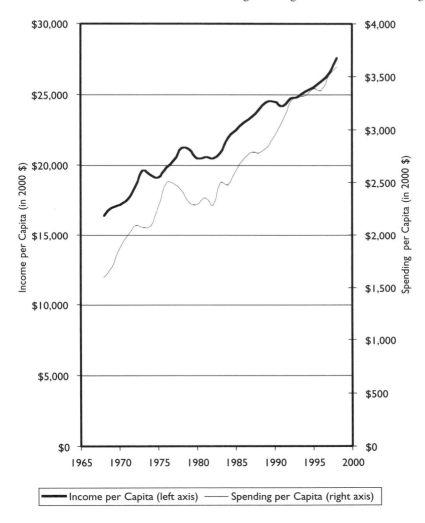

Fig. 7.1. State spending growth compared to income growth, 1969–98

eral spending as a share of U.S. income equaled 24 percent, reached a peak of 28 percent in 1983, and then began a downward trend. Federal spending declined to 22 percent in 1998, below its 1969 level. In the mid-1980s, the paths of state and federal spending parted ways; state spending continued its upward march even as federal spending trended downward. Thus, while the size of the federal government sector in relation to income remained considerably larger than the

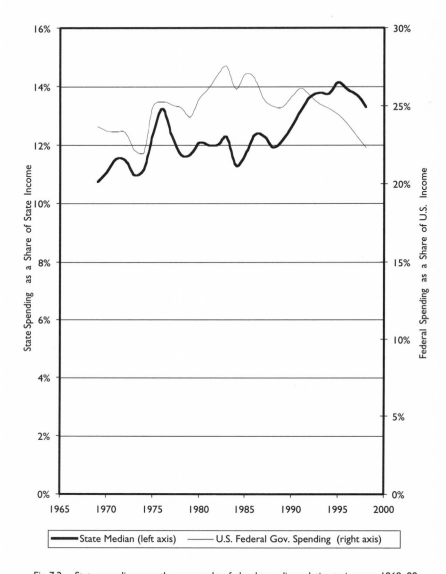

Fig. 7.2.   State spending growth compared to federal spending relative to income, 1969–98

typical state government sector, state spending increased relative to income while federal spending did not.[3]

The splurge in government spending was not uniform among the states. Figure 7.3 ranks the states in terms of growth in state spending per capita between 1969 and 1998 (adjusted for inflation in 2000 dollars). Figure 7.4 ranks the states in terms of growth in spending as a share of state income. New Jersey experienced the largest spending growth by either measure, growing 114 percent in per capita terms and 61 percent in relation to income. Nevada experienced the smallest growth in state spending per capita, 39 percent. Figure 7.4 shows that in only two states, Nevada and Vermont, did income growth outpace state spending growth over these three decades. Virginia, the median state in terms of per capita spending growth, grew 75 percent and Florida, the median state in terms of spending as a share of income growth, grew 25 percent.

What accounts for this vast disparity in the growth of spending among the states? The simple convergence thesis merits some attention. In this view, competition among states would motivate policymakers in low-spending states to match the programs and services offered in high-spending states. Policymakers in high-spending (and therefore high-revenue) states would be motivated to constrain government growth to bring the tax burden in closer accord with the relatively low-spending, low-tax states. The relevance of these convergence forces can be seen in figure 7.5, which plots the average level of spending per capita in 1968 and 1969 (in logged form) on the horizontal axis and the growth in real per capita spending (1969–98) on the vertical axis. The obvious negative pattern in these data suggests the presence of a convergence process. For example, Nevada and Vermont, which experienced the slowest growth in government spending over the period, were among the states with the highest level of per capita spending in 1968–69. New Jersey, which experienced the fastest per capita spending growth (116 percent), had the fourth smallest level of per capita spending in 1968–69.

Figure 7.6 plots this convergence relationship using state spending as a share of income, and again the data pattern clearly indicates the negative trade-off. By and large, states with large governments in the late 1960s tended toward slow growth and states with initially small governments tended toward rapid growth over the next three decades.

The convergence pattern in state government spending can be exposited using the alternative and more rigorous technique shown in

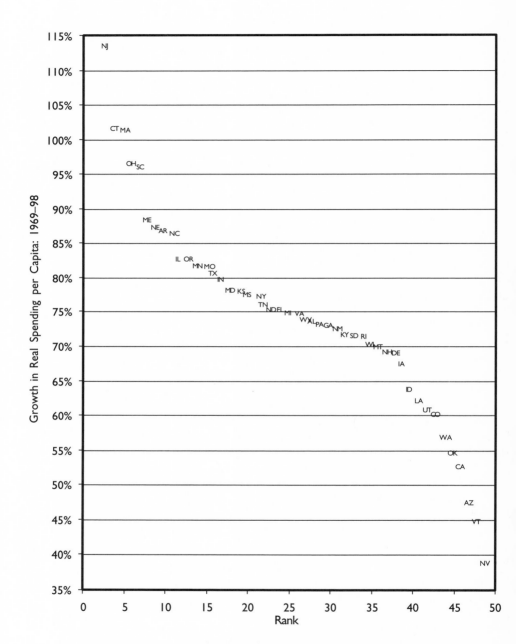

Fig. 7.3. Comparison of state spending growth, 1969–98 (ranked by growth in real spending per capita)

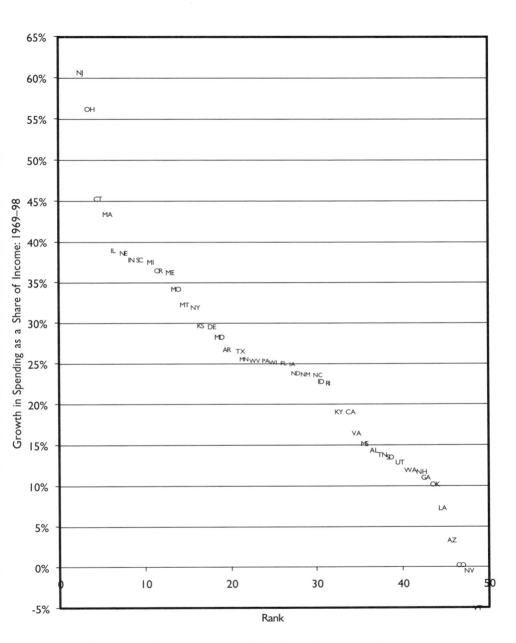

Fig. 7.4.   Comparison of state spending growth, 1969–98 (ranked by growth in spending relative to income)

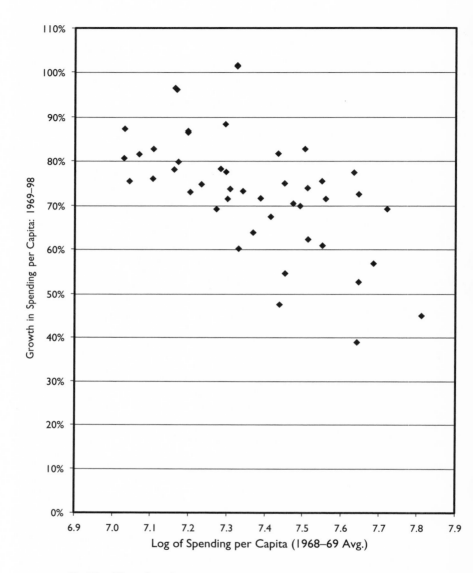

Fig. 7.5.   Effect of initial government size on growth in spending per capita

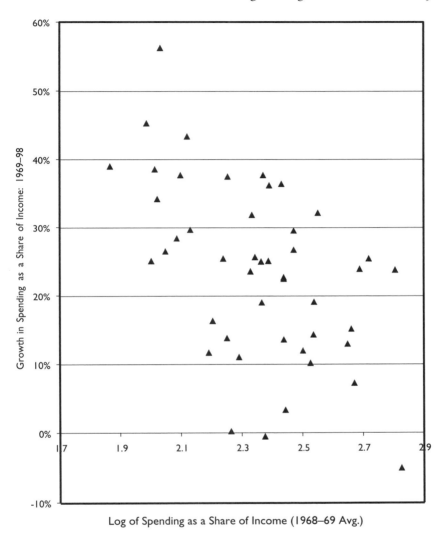

Fig. 7.6.   Effect of initial government size on growth in spending relative to income

figures 7.7 and 7.8. Figure 7.7 plots the coefficient of variation in spending per capita, and figure 7.8 plots the coefficient of variation in spending as a share of income. The dispersion in spending per capita across states dropped 32 percent, from 0.029 in 1968 to 0.019 in 1998. Similarly, the dispersion in spending as a share of income across

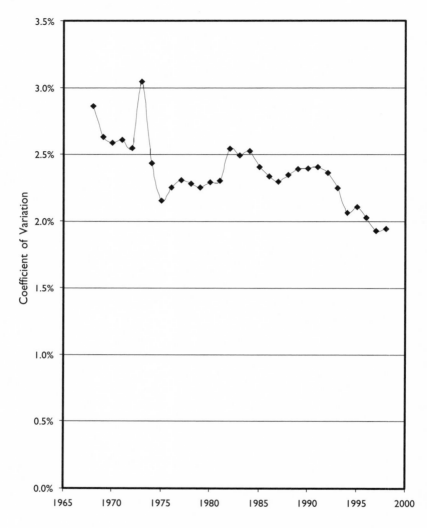

Fig. 7.7.   Convergence among states in spending per capita

states dropped 33 percent, from 0.11 in 1968 to 0.07 in 1998. In sum, a process of interstate fiscal competition appears to play a pertinent role in driving aggregate spending policies over the course of the three decades. It is important to note that the forces of convergence over the two-decade period, 1977–98, appear far less impressive. For example, the dispersion in spending as a share of income in 1998

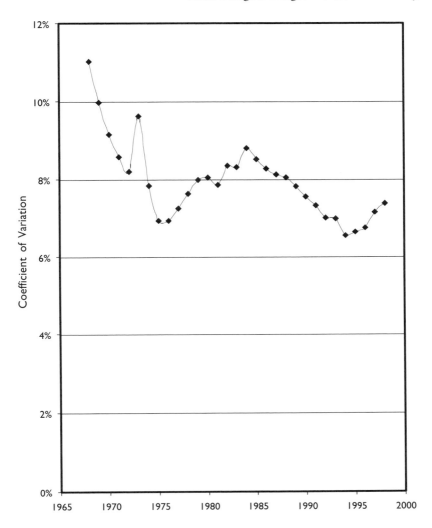

Fig. 7.8.   Convergence among states in spending as a share of income

equaled its value in 1977 (see fig. 7.8). Likewise, figure 7.7 shows that much of the convergence in spending per capita occurred in the early 1970s. Spending dispersion remained almost flat for 20 years, from 1975 until 1994.

Figure 7.9 illustrates changes in spending levels for the individual states by comparing spending per capita in the late 1990s to the levels three decades earlier. The states' rankings in terms of average

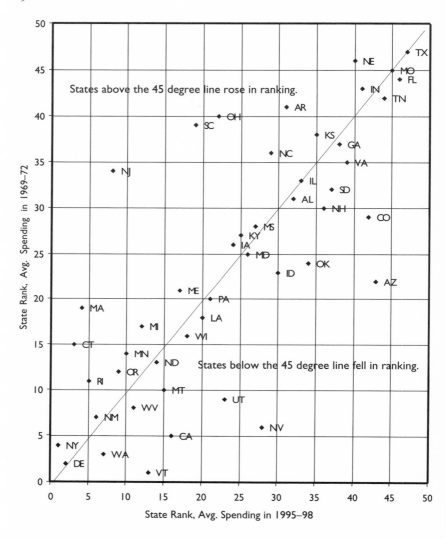

Fig. 7.9.   Changes in relative spending over three decades (1 = highest spending per capita; 50 = lowest spending per capita)

spending per capita in the 1995–98 period are shown on the horizontal axis, and the states' rankings in the 1969–72 period are shown on the vertical axis. The state with the largest spending receives a rank of 1, and the state with the smallest spending receives a rank of 47.[4] New York tops the list in the late 1990s (with spending equal to

$5,016 per capita), followed by Delaware, Connecticut, Massachusetts, and Rhode Island. Clearly states in the Northeastern region of the United States tend to be the big spenders by this measure. At the other end of the scale, Texas had the lowest per capita spending in the late 1990s ($2,703 per capita), followed by Florida, Missouri, Tennessee, and Arizona.

Figure 7.10 also ranks the states in terms of spending, in this case measuring government size in spending as a share of state income. Again rankings are provided for 1995–98 (the horizontal axis) and for 1969–72 (the vertical axis). Using this indicator, New Mexico had the highest spending in the late 1990s (20 percent of state income), followed by West Virginia, Montana, North Dakota, and Mississippi. Note that this indicator of state government size yields a quite different ranking than that based on per capita spending, as shown in figure 7.9; Northeastern states no longer dominate the high end of the spending scale. Colorado had the lowest spending as a share of income in the late 1990s (10 percent of state income), followed by Florida, Illinois, New Hampshire, and Texas. The contrast in the state rankings shown in these two figures reveals that these two commonly used indicators of the size of government provide materially different conclusions.

Figures 7.9 and 7.10 make it easy to identify the extent to which the relative size of state governments remained constant over the 1969–98 period. States for which relative state spending remained unchanged over these three decades fall along the 45 degree line. For example, in figure 7.9 Texas falls on the 45 degree line in the top right corner, indicating that Texas ranks as the lowest spender in per capita terms at the beginning and at the end of the three decades. Delaware falls on the 45 degree line in the bottom left corner, indicating that Delaware continued to hold the second biggest spender spot throughout the three decades. Only two other states maintained the same relative spending ranking, Illinois and Missouri.

State government spending per capita in New Jersey gained the most ground in relation to other states. New Jersey rose from thirty-fourth position in the early 1960s to eighth position in the late 1990s. Note that this result conforms to the growth rankings in figure 7.4, which showed that government spending in New Jersey grew more than in any other state. The second biggest increase in spending per capita occurred in South Carolina, which moved ahead of 20 states, from thirty-ninth rank to nineteenth rank.

More generally, figure 7.9 identifies the states in which spending

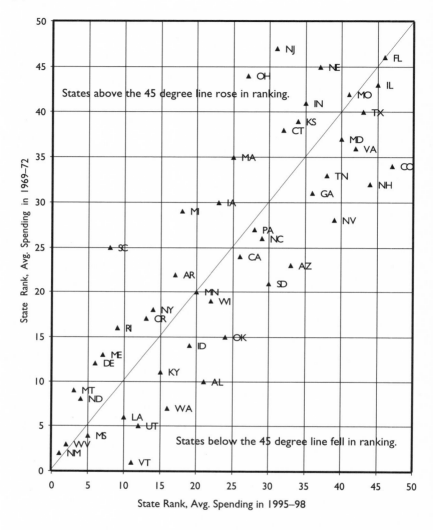

Fig. 7.10.   Changes in relative spending over three decades (1 = highest spending relative to income; 50 = lowest spending relative to income)

increased relative to other states as those lying above the 45 degree line, where a greater distance from the 45 degree line indicates a larger relative increase in spending. Symmetrically, the states in which spending decreased relative to other states lie below the 45 degree line. On that front, Nevada experienced the largest relative spending decrease, dropping below 22 states, from the sixth position to the twenty-eighth position. Figure 7.10 provides the identical analysis, ranking the states based on spending as a share of state income as an alternative indicator of government size. By that measure, Ohio shows the largest increase in spending relative to other states. Colorado shows the largest decrease in spending relative to other states.

Commentary

The outburst of federal debt in the 1970s and even more in the 1980s drew considerable media attention and perhaps diverted attention away from state fiscal developments. By comparison to federal fiscal events, state governments seemed to be performing relatively well, especially with regard to debt-financed expenditures. What seems to have been lost on most observers is that the growth of federal spending reversed course in the mid-1980s; yet in the typical state spending continued to grow almost 1 percentage point faster than income for the remainder of the twentieth century. In fact, the growth in state government spending failed to outpace income growth in only two states (Vermont and Nevada) in the final three decades of the twentieth century.

The data in this chapter reveal extensive diversity among states with respect to the size and growth in state government spending. A simple convergence thesis explains some but not much of the spending diversity among states, particularly in the years after 1975. Chapters 8 and 9 proceed to investigate in considerable detail the economic, demographic, institutional, and ideological factors that appear to explain these wide variations in state spending patterns.

Chapter 8

Fiscal Uncertainty: The Enemy of Efficient Budgeting

This chapter analyzes, or in some cases updates and reanalyzes, the impact of fiscal institutions on state fiscal policy. The conclusions about certain fiscal institutions generally conform to those in prior studies. However, conducting the empirical analysis with a uniform set of control variables and within a common time period facilitates a comparison of the relative impact of various institutions.[1]

The chapter breaks new ground in several respects. Like prior studies, the models examine the impact of institutions on the size of government, looking at spending, revenues, and taxes. Beyond that, the analysis examines both theoretically and empirically the relationship between fiscal volatility and state spending. Fiscal volatility creates uncertainty with respect to future operations of government agencies, and this impedes the selection of efficient production processes. This extension of the mean-variance perspective to state fiscal performance adds another dimension to the study of fiscal institutions. The models proceed to examine the impact of institutions on the volatility of state budgets and through this channel their indirect effects on the size of government.

Fiscal Volatility and the Size of Government

The analysis seeks to explore a new dimension in fiscal policy: the relationship between the predictability of government budgets and their size.[2] Elementary economic theory teaches us that, to minimize production costs, factors such as land, labor, and capital will be employed in accord with their marginal productivities relative to their marginal costs. The particular input mix that yields the greatest efficiency depends in part on the available technology, on the speed with which factors employed in production may be adjusted, and on how much output flexibility is required. Technology-related constraints are typically handled by the analytical distinction between short-run and long-run adjustment paths. Given a sufficient time to adjust all factors, capital investments will be made to adopt the cost-minimizing technology to produce any level of output. The degree of flexibility required typically depends on how widely demand fluctuates over time. These two temporal elements may clash, and this adds a crucial element into the choice of an optimal production process.

The trade-off between output volatility and efficiency is described with reference to figure 8.1. Consider a government agency planning its future operations for the next two fiscal years, FY_1 and FY_2. By assumption this agency seeks to minimize operating costs, including all capital costs. The agency must select one of two alternative production processes, the α-process or the β-process. Figure 8.1 shows the total cost functions associated with these two processes, labeled TC_α and TC_β, assumed for simplicity to be linear. These total cost relationships characterize the agency's operations in each fiscal year. The β-process requires a larger locked-in investment than the α-process, and by assumption this investment is irreversible over the two-year planning horizon. These different capital requirements mean that the marginal costs under the α-process exceed marginal costs under the β-process, which is reflected by the relative slopes of the two total cost functions. For example, the α-process can accommodate output reversals more efficiently than the β-process because it embraces short-term leases rather than constructing new facilities or it performs functions in-house rather than committing to long-term outsourcing contracts.

Under the budget process posited here, the agency knows its expected output in the initial fiscal period labeled Q_1 in figure 8.1. By construction, the cost of producing Q_1 is the same, $600 million, using either the α-process or the β-process. The agency's decision to adopt the α-process or the β-process thus depends on its expected output in FY_2. Let Q_L and Q_H stand for two possible outcomes in FY_2, the first reflecting a lower output and the second reflecting a higher output relative to Q_1. If high output level Q_H were known with certainty, the β-process would be more efficient than the α-process and therefore selected. If the low output level Q_L were known with certainty, the α-process would be selected.

In contrast to these two certain outcomes, suppose the agency as an integral part of its planning exercise must predict the probability of Q_L or Q_H. To make the analysis as simple as possible, suppose Q_L and Q_H are equally probable, or Prob $(Q_L) = 0.5$ and Prob $(Q_H) = 0.5$. This means of course that the agency can do no better than to choose a process randomly and that the wrong process (that is, the

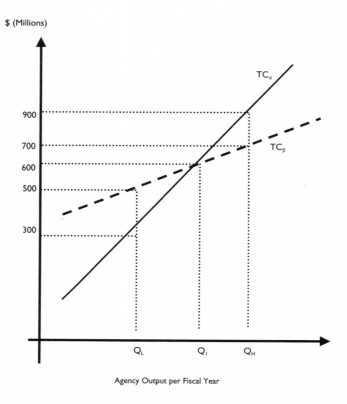

$ (Millions)

TC$_\alpha$

900

700   TC$_\beta$

600

500

300

Q$_L$ Q$_I$ Q$_H$

Agency Output per Fiscal Year

Fig. 8.1.   Uncertainty of future funding levels and agency costs

process that would not yield the lowest cost) will be selected half of the time. Under this uncertain fiscal environment, the agency's expected costs would be $100 million higher than they would be under a certain fiscal environment. That is, with probability 0.5 the agency's random choice proves correct, either selecting the α-process and Q$_L$ materializes or selecting the β-process and Q$_H$ materializes. With probability 0.5 the agency's choice proves incorrect, and given an incorrect choice, costs exceed the minimum cost level by $200 million.[3]

As this simple model illustrates, uncertainty about future output rates conveys risks associated with long-run operations relative to a more predictable fiscal environment. The empirical models presented later in the chapter explore whether and to what extent the postulated trade-off between volatility and efficiency systematically affects government spending levels.

Mechanisms for Fiscal Discipline: Which Fiscal Rules Work?

Shaped by a century of presidential appeals for an item veto of appropriations measures and of pleas for a balanced budget amendment to the Constitution, much of the debate about budget process reform at the U.S. federal level has concentrated on these two institutions.[4] Naturally, the differences among states with respect to these two institutions invite empirical scrutiny. These and three other institutions that have been identified in prior research as potentially important are briefly described, and the next section examines the impact of these institutions on state fiscal outcomes. As previewed in the introduction to this chapter, the empirical section investigates the direct effects on spending levels (the standard approach in the literature) and the indirect effects on fiscal volatility.

Balanced Budget Rules

Every state except Vermont has a balanced budget requirement. However, the details of these 49 state requirements differ in an important respect, namely, the stage in the budget process at which balance is required. A survey of past research points to four categories of requirements. The weakest standard requires the governor to submit a balanced budget. A stricter standard requires the legislature to pass a balanced budget. Under these two categories actual expenditures may exceed revenues if end-of-year realizations happen to diverge from the enacted budget. The third standard requires the state to acknowledge its deficit but allows the deficit to be carried over into the next budget with no consequences. Bohn and Inman (1996) aptly label these three categories "prospective budget constraints." The fourth and strictest form of balanced budget rule combines the practice of enacting a balanced budget with a prohibition on a deficit carryforward. Bohn and Inman label this strictest form a "retrospective budget constraint." While numerous studies have examined state balanced budget rules, three studies convincingly advance the idea that the retrospective standard has a significant impact on fiscal policy, whereas the other three do not.

Bohn and Inman find that balanced budget rules that prohibit the carryover of end-of-year budget deficits have a statistically significant effect, reducing state general fund deficits by $100 per person. In contrast, soft or prospective budget constraints on proposed budgets do not affect deficits. Moreover, the deficit reduction in retrospective budget constraint states comes through lower levels of spending and not through higher tax revenues.

Poterba (1994) examines the fiscal responses in states to unexpected deficits or surpluses. He compares the adjustments to fiscal shocks under "weak" versus "strict" antideficit rules, categories that closely resemble the Bohn-Inman division. Poterba's results suggest that states with weak antideficit rules adjust less to shocks than states with strict rules. A $100 deficit per person overrun leads to only a $17 per person expenditure cut in a state with a weak rule and to a $44 cut in states with strict rules. Poterba also finds no evidence that antideficit rules affect the magnitude of tax changes in the aftermath of an unexpected deficit.

Alt and Lowry (1994) focus on the role of political partisanship in fiscal policy. They examine reactions to disparities between revenues and expenditures that can exist even in states with balanced budget requirements. In states that prohibit deficit carryovers, the party in control matters. In Republican-controlled states, they find that a one dollar state deficit triggers a 77¢ response through tax increases or spending reductions. In Democrat-controlled states a one dollar deficit triggers a 34¢ reaction. In states that do not prohibit carryovers, the adjustments are 31¢ (Republicans) and 40¢ (Democrats). This evidence suggests that state politics plays an important role and that antideficit rules affect fiscal actions.

Following these important studies, the empirical analysis focuses on the effects of strict balanced budget requirements, those that prohibit deficit carryovers from one fiscal year to the next.

The Item Reduction Veto

Governors in all but five states have the ability to veto a particular item in an appropriations bill, in addition to their normal authority to veto an entire bill. Several studies on the fiscal impact of the item veto provide mixed and inconclusive results. Bohn and Inman (1996) find that the item veto generally has no statistically significant relationship to state general fund surpluses or deficits. Carter and Schap (1990) find no systematic effect of the item veto on state spending. Holtz-Eakin (1988) finds that when government power is divided between the two parties, one controlling the executive branch and the other controlling the legislative branch, the item veto helps the governor reduce spending and raise taxes. Holtz-Eakin finds that, under political conditions of nondivided government, the item veto yields little, if any, effect.

The Holtz-Eakin study stressed that the item veto powers differ among states, and Crain and Miller (1990) examine these different powers in further detail. They find that, in contrast to a generic classification of the item veto, a particular form of the item veto—the so-called item reduction veto—significantly reduces spending growth. Of the 45 states that have an item veto, 10 give their governors the authority to either write in a lower spending level or veto the entire item. The Crain and Miller article argues that the item reduction veto differs from the standard item veto because it provides the governor with superior agenda-setting authority. For example, a governor faced with excessive funding for a remedial reading program is unlikely to veto the measure but likely would consider a marginal reduction in the amount of funding for that type of program. Based on this finding, the analysis examines in new detail the fiscal impact of the item reduction veto.

Tax and Expenditure Limitations

The earliest studies of tax and expenditure limitations (TELs) concluded that they have virtually no effect on state fiscal policy (e.g., Abrams and Dougan 1986). Elder (1992) was among the first studies to examine TELs using an empirical model that controlled for other factors (such as income and population) that influence spending. With this improved specification Elder finds evidence that TELs reduce the growth of state government.

Eichengreen (1992) estimates regression models for both the level and the growth rate in state spending as a function of the presence of tax and expenditure limits and the interaction between these limits and the state's personal income growth rate. He finds that the interaction term is particularly important because limits are typically specified as a fraction of personal income. In states with slow income growth rates, limitation laws have had a more restrictive effect on government growth than in states with fast income growth rates. Shadbegian (1996) specifies an almost identical empirical model, again taking into consideration the interaction between state income and TELs.

Reuben (1995) develops an empirical specification that controls for the potential endogeneity problem that the passage of tax limits may be related to a state's fiscal conditions. Reuben finds that when these institutions are treated as endogenous the explanatory power of the institutional variables rises markedly; the estimated effects indicate that TELs significantly reduce state spending.

Supermajority Voting Requirement for Tax Increases

Knight (2000) points out that, in addition to the 12 states that have enacted supermajority requirements, 16 states have introduced proposals to enact such requirements. Adding a supermajority voting requirement to the U.S. federal budget process is also a popular reform measure. Two empirical studies have analyzed the effect of supermajority requirements on state fiscal outcomes. Crain and Miller (1990) find that such rules reduce the growth in state spending by about 2 percent based on a relatively short sample period, 1980–86. The study by Knight (2000) expands the sample period; employs pooled time-series, cross-sectional data; and uses state and year fixed-effects variables. He finds that supermajority requirements decrease the level of taxes by about 8 percent relative to the mean level of state taxes.

Budget Cycles

Since 1977 a number of proposals have been introduced in the U.S. House and Senate to lengthen the federal budget cycle from an annual to a biennial process. The perception behind these proposals is that a federal biennial budget would help curtail the growth of federal expenditures. Motivated by these federal proposals, the U.S. General Accounting Office (1987) conducted a study of the state experiences. That study reports a positive correlation between state spending and annual budget cycles.[5]

Kearns (1994) lays out the theoretical issues and provides the most comprehensive empirical study of state budget cycles to date. Kearns presents two competing hypotheses. On the one hand, a biennial budget transfers power over fiscal decisions from the legislative branch to the governor. This power transfer reduces spending activities associated with logrolling and pork barrel politics because legislators favor programs that benefit their narrow, geographically based constituencies. The main costs of such geographically targeted programs may be exported to nonconstituents. By comparison, the governor makes fiscal decisions based on more inclusive benefit-cost calculations because he or she represents a broader, statewide constituency. In other words, at-large representation mitigates the fiscal commons problem. Offering an alternative hypothesis, Kearns posits that a biennial budget cycle imparts durability to spending decisions and thereby encourages political pressure groups to seek government programs.[6] Kearns concludes in favor of the latter thesis based on her finding that states with biennial budgets have higher spending per capita than states with annual budgets.

A third and original hypothesis derives from the conceptual framework developed in the prior section. Namely, lengthening the budget cycle adds predictability to agency funding levels, facilitating the development and execution of efficient operating plans.

Model Specification Issues and Empirical Results

The empirical model to investigate the impact of fiscal volatility and fiscal institutions is developed in three steps beginning with equation (8.1).

$$\text{Expenditure}_{it} = \Phi X_{it} + \alpha_i + \tau_t + \varepsilon_{it}. \tag{8.1}$$

The estimates use two forms of the dependent variable, Expenditure_{it}: one divides state spending by state personal income, and the other divides state spending by state population. The expenditure per capita variable and all dollar-denominated variables used in the models are adjusted for inflation using 2000 prices as the base year. The data sample pools time-series and cross-sectional data, the variable subscript i denotes an observation on an individual state, and the subscript t denotes an observation in a particular year. α_i represents a set of state dummy variables, one for each state in the sample, and τ_t represents a set of time dummy variables, one for each year in the sample.

In equation (8.1) X_{it} represents a vector of variables that control for economic and demographic factors that influence state government spending. These variables include income per capita, the unemployment rate, population, the percentage of the population residing in urban areas, and the percentage of the population between the ages of 18 and 64. This set of control variables fairly represents the variables in prior studies on state spending, and the underlying rationale requires only brief explanation.[7] Income per capita proxies both the demand for public sector services as well as the size of the potential tax base. The unemployment rate proxies potential claims for unemployment insurance and related welfare programs. Population controls for economies of scale in publicly provided services, and per capita costs predictably fall as population increases. Similarly, per capita costs should fall in states with largely urban, relatively concentrated populations. The variable for the percentage of the population between the ages of 18 and 64 is included because young residents (less than 18 years old) and elderly residents (more than 64 years old) generate the greatest demands for public education, health care, and other social services. Thus this variable should vary inversely with government spending.

Of course, other factors such as climatic conditions or foreign immigration may cause spending to differ among the states. The α_i (fixed-effects) dummy variables will control for such state-specific factors to the extent that they remain roughly constant over the sample period. Finally, the τ_t (year-effects) dummy variables control for influences on state spending such as a national recession, changes in federal grant programs, or changes in the federal tax code.

The sample for estimating equation (8.1) includes 47 states (Alaska, Hawaii, and Wyoming are excluded) for the years 1970 through 1998. Table 8.A1 in the appendix at the end of this chapter provides summary statistics for the variables and data sources.

Table 8.1 shows the results of estimating equation (8.1) using the two measures of state expenditures: expenditures as a share of income (Model 1) and expenditures per capita (Model 2). All the parameter estimates show the expected signs, and the models are estimated with a high degree of precision, as indicated by the high adjusted R-squared values and significant F-statistics. The Income per Capita variable has a positive correlation with Expenditures per Capita but a negative correlation with Expenditures as a Share of Income. This reflects the fact that state spending generally rises or falls with state income, but less than proportionately. State spending varies positively with the unemployment rate. Large states and states with largely urban populations experience lower spending (per capita and as a share of income) than other states, consistent with the economies of scale thesis. Spending declines with the share of a state's population between the ages of 18 and 64, or, to restate this relationship more intuitively, spending rises as the share of the population that is young or old grows. Finally, all of the τ_t coefficients for the year dummy variables (not reported in the table) are significant.

The analysis next augments this basic model to include the main variables of interest, beginning with expenditure volatility. This extension is shown in equation (8.2):

$$\text{Expenditure}_{it} = \lambda \sigma_i + \Phi X_{it} + \tau_t + \varphi_{it}. \tag{8.2}$$

The additional variable denoted σ_i measures the volatility in state spending. σ_i is the standard deviation of ε_{it}, the residuals from the models estimated using equation (8.1). That is, these residuals represent the deviations in spending from the values predicted based on the variables in X_{it}, τ_t, and α_i. This specification assumes that σ_i differs across states but not across time for an individual state and that $\varepsilon_{it} \sim N(0, \sigma_i^2)$. Consistent with the previous analysis, two alternative measures are computed, one reflecting spending as a share of income and the other reflecting spending per capita.

Equation (8.3) shows the third step in the estimation procedure, extending the basic framework to include institutional variables:

$$\text{Expenditure}_{it} = \beta P_{it} + \lambda \sigma_i + \Phi X_{it} + \tau_t + \varphi_{it}. \tag{8.3}$$

Here P_{it} represents a vector of five institutional variables: a Strict Balanced Budget Requirement (i.e., one that does not allow deficit carryovers), the Item Reduction Veto, a Supermajority Voting Requirement for a Tax Increase, Tax and Expenditure Limitations, and a Biennial Budget Cycle.

Equation (8.3) is estimated as a cross-sectional time-series linear (or panel) model using a feasible generalized least squares technique.

TABLE 8.1. Core Variables Used to Explain State Government Expenditures

Independent Variables	Dependent Variable = Expenditures as a Share of Income	Dependent Variable = per Capita[a] Expenditures
	Model 1	Model 2
Income per Capita[a]	−0.000002	0.068
	(−9.72)**	(13.13)**
Unemployment Rate[b]	0.001	20
	(4.92)**	(4.49)**
ln (Population)	−0.027	−696
	(−9.34)**	(−10.95)**
Urban Population (% of	−0.0004	−14
population)[b]	(−2.51)**	(−3.88)**
Population Age 18 to 64	−0.002	−34
(% of population)[b]	(−5.05)**	(−4.57)**
Year dummy variables	Yes	Yes
State fixed effects	Yes	Yes
R-squared, within states	0.61	0.90
R-squared, between states	0.30	0.03
R-squared, overall	0.31	0.24
F-statistic	61.9**	361**
Total panel observations[c]	1,363	1,363

Note: t-statistics are shown in parentheses.
[a]Denominated in real (2000) dollars.
[b]Variables denominated as fractions are multiplied by 100 in the estimation models.
[c]Sample includes 47 states for the years 1970–98. Alaska, Hawaii, and Wyoming are omitted.
* Indicates significance at the 5 percent level for a two-tailed test. ** Indicates significance at the 1 percent level for a two-tailed test.

The specific procedure used iterates the GLS estimation technique to convergence. The FGLS technique allows estimation in the presence of autocorrelation within states and cross-sectional heteroskedasticity across states. The FGLS estimation procedure estimates and then adjusts for systematic patterns in the residuals across states.

Results for Fiscal Volatility

The results of estimating equation (8.3) are divided into two tables. Table 8.2 reports the models that use Expenditures per Capita as the dependent variable. In these models the Expenditure Volatility variable is computed based on the deviations in expenditures per capita. Table 8.3 reports the models that use Expenditures as a Share of Income as the dependent variable. In these models the Expenditure Volatility variable is computed based on the deviations in expendi-

TABLE 8.2.   Effects of Fiscal Institutions on State Government Expenditures per Capita

Independent Variables	Dependent Variable = Expenditures per Capita		
	FGLS	FGLS	Two-Stage Estimate
Expenditure Volatility[a]	2.22	2.51	5.87
	(14.25)**	(17.51)**	(17.49)**
Strict Balanced Budget Requirement	—	−237	−88
(= 1 if yes)		(−10.60)**	(−3.57)**
Item Reduction Veto Power (= 1 if yes)	—	−281	−377
		(−15.52)**	(−14.54)**
Supermaj. Required for Tax Increase	—	−240	−121
(= 1 if yes)		(−9.37)**	(−5.50)**
Tax or Expenditure Limitation (TEL)	—	−1567	−1173
(= 1 if yes)		(−12.45)**	(−10.27)**
Interaction Term: TEL × Income per	—	0.073	0.061
Capita		(13.20)**	(12.37)**
Biennial Budget Cycle (= 1 if yes)	—	13	95
		(0.80)	(5.86)**
Year dummy variables	Yes	Yes	Yes
Other variables included, see table 8.1	Model 2	Model 2	Model 2
Wald chi-squared	5364**	7407**	7658**
Total panel observations[b]	1,363	1,363	1,363

Note: Parameters are estimated using cross-sectional time-series FGLS regressions. *z*-statistics are shown in parentheses.

[a]Expenditure Volatility is measured as the standard deviation in the regression residuals from the core model referenced in table 8.1.

[b]Sample includes 47 states for the years 1970–98. Alaska, Hawaii, and Wyoming are omitted.

* Indicates significance at the 5 percent level for a two-tailed test. ** Indicates significance at the 1 percent level for a two-tailed test.

tures as a share of income. The model specifications reported in these two tables are otherwise identical. To avoid repetition, the results in tables 8.2 and 8.3 do not report the estimated coefficients for the vector of control variables (income, unemployment, population, urbanization, and population age); the parameter estimates on these variables appear robust with respect to the various model specifications.

A final element of the estimation strategy requires clarification before proceeding to the results. Because the institutional variables of interest may affect Expenditure Volatility as well as the level of Expenditures, the parameter estimates based on a single equation model (FGLS) may be biased. To take this potential endogeneity bias into account, the coefficients in equation (8.3) are also estimated using a two-stage method that endogenizes the Expenditure Volatility measures.

TABLE 8.3. Effects of Fiscal Institutions on State Government Expenditures as a Share of Income

Independent Variables	Dependent Variable = Expenditures as a Share of State Income		
	FGLS	FGLS	Two-Stage Estimate
Expenditure Volatility[a]	2.77	2.80	6.21
	(19.66)**	(19.33)**	(22.07)**
Strict Balanced Budget Requirement	—	−0.008	−0.004
(= 1 if yes)		(−7.57)**	(−3.39)*
Item Reduction Veto Power (= 1 if yes)	—	−0.012	−0.014
		(−13.89)**	(−13.14)**
Supermaj. Required for Tax Increase	—	−0.009	−0.010
(= 1 if yes)		(−7.66)**	(−10.00)**
Tax or Expenditure Limitation (TEL)	—	−0.066	−0.048
(= 1 if yes)		(−11.99)**	(−9.25)**
Interaction Term: TEL × Income per	—	0.000003	0.000002
Capita		(12.68)**	(10.86)**
Biennial Budget Cycle (= 1 if yes)	—	−0.001	0.001
		(−1.37)	(1.35)
Year dummy variables	Yes	Yes	Yes
Other variables included, see table 8.1	Model 1	Model 1	Model 1
Wald chi-squared	2624**	3317**	3698**
Total panel observations[b]	1,363	1,363	1,363

Note: Parameters are estimated using cross-sectional time-series FGLS regressions. z-statistics are shown in parentheses.

[a]Expenditure Volatility is measured as the standard deviation in the regression residuals from the core model referenced in table 8.1.

[b]Sample includes 47 states for the years 1972–98. Alaska, Hawaii, and Wyoming are omitted.

* Indicates significance at the 5 percent level for a two-tailed test. ** Indicates significance at the 1 percent level for a two-tailed test.

The first stage obtains the predicted value of Expenditure Volatility based on the other right-hand side variables, and the second stage uses this predicted valued in the estimation.[8] Tables 8.2 and 8.3 provide both the single equation FGLS and the two-stage estimation results for comparison.

The first columns in tables 8.2 and 8.3 present the results for equation (8.2), that is, when only the Expenditure Volatility variable is added to the core model, specified in equation (8.1). The estimated coefficient on Expenditure Volatility is positive and significant at the 1 percent level in these two models. Expenditure Volatility is also significant at the 1 percent level in the other models shown in tables 8.2 and 8.3 that include the additional institutional variables. These results strongly support the conceptual framework laid out earlier in the chapter. Namely, fiscal uncertainty impairs efficiency and raises the cost of government programs.

The size of the impact of Expenditure Volatility on spending can be illustrated using the per capita results in the third column of results in table 8.2. In that (two-stage) model the estimated coefficient for Expenditure Volatility is 5.87.[9] Consider a 10 percent increase in Expenditure Volatility from its mean value of $162 (a 10 percent increase in volatility equals about $16 per capita). The projected impact would be a $95 increase in per capita spending (= 5.87 × $16). Using the mean value of per capita spending (= $2,724 for the 1970–98 period), this represents a 3.5 percent increase in per capita spending (= $95/$2,724). This point estimate evaluated at the mean implies an elasticity of per capita spending with respect to spending volatility of 0.35. As a second illustration of the magnitude of the uncertainty-efficiency trade-off, suppose Expenditure Volatility rises by one standard deviation (= $68). The projected impact would be to increase per capita spending by $400 (= 5.87 × $68), a 15 percent increase relative to the spending mean (= $400/$2,724). Figure 8.2 illustrates graphically this estimated trade-off between budget volatility and per capita spending. Figure 8.3 illustrates the trade-off using the estimated results for spending as a share of income (from table 8.3).

Of course, this link between volatility and spending can be framed in a constructive manner: a state may reap substantial budgetary savings by reducing fiscal volatility. The subsequent analysis explores further the determinants of spending volatility, including the potential role of fiscal institutions and the volatility of state tax revenues.

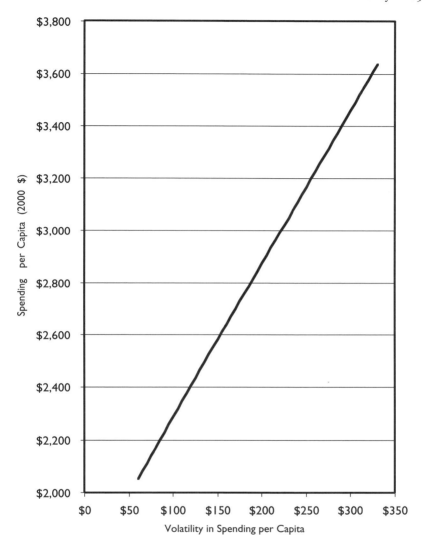

Fig. 8.2.   Trade-off between budget volatility and spending per capita

Results for Fiscal Institutions

The results in tables 8.2 and 8.3 indicate that fiscal institutions also exert significant influences on state spending. With one exception (the Biennial Budget Cycle variable) the estimated coefficients on the institutional variables are significant at the 1 percent level. Again,

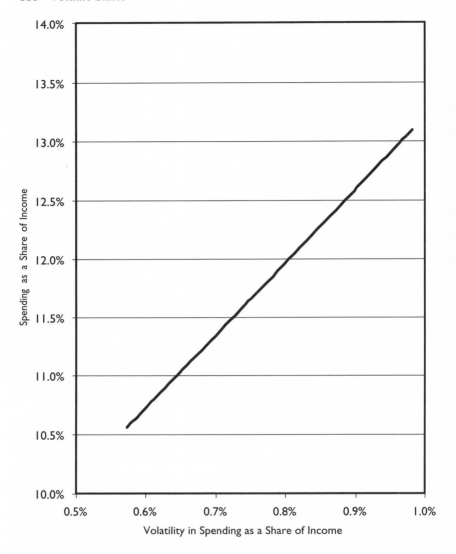

Fig. 8.3.   Trade-off between budget volatility and spending as a share of income

the impact of these institutions can be illustrated using the per capita results in table 8.2 (the two-stage model). First, states that have a Strict Balanced Budget Requirement (that is, a deficit cannot be carried over to the next fiscal year) spend on average $88 per capita less than other states, or about 3.2 percent less in relation to the mean of per capita spending (= $88/$2,724). Note that when this model is estimated using the one-stage FGLS (the second column of results in table 8.2) the estimated impact is a $237 reduction in per capita spending, or an 8 percent reduction in relation to the mean. This large difference between the one- and two-stage estimates exposes the potential importance of untangling the direct and the indirect effects of fiscal institutions. A Strict Balanced Budget Requirement has an impact on budget stability and through that channel has an indirect effect on government spending.

The findings for the Item Reduction Veto indicate that this authority has major consequences. Granting the governor an Item Reduction Veto predictably lowers per capita spending by $377, or about 13 percent relative to the mean (= $377/$2,724). Interestingly and unlike the results for the balanced budget rule, here the single equation estimates predict a smaller impact on spending ($281 per capita) than the endogenous estimates ($377 per capita), a 34 percent difference between the two estimates of this parameter. As this large difference suggests, the Item Reduction Veto contributes to budget volatility, and this indirect effect offsets at least in part its direct contribution to spending restraint. The Supermajority Voting Requirement for a Tax Increase lowers per capita spending by $121, or about 4 percent evaluated at the sample mean. Here again the endogenous estimate is about half the magnitude of the single equation estimate, which strongly indicates that fiscal institutions play a two-dimensional role, influencing budget volatility as well as the level of spending.

The effect of Tax and Expenditure Limitation rules needs to be assessed using both the coefficients of the dummy variable and its interaction term with state income, both of which are statistically significant. As in prior studies that employ this methodology (e.g., Eichengreen 1992; Shadbegian 1996) the coefficient on the interaction term is positive. This means that changes in state spending are more responsive to changes in income in TEL states compared to non-TEL states. This increase in responsiveness is not surprising because most TELs explicitly tie spending or revenue growth to state economic conditions. If we evaluate the effect at the mean of per capita income, the projection indicates that spending per capita is $168 higher (6 percent) with a TEL than without one. If a state's income were one standard deviation below the mean, a TEL would reduce per capita spending by $91, about 3 percent in relation to mean spending. Alternatively, if a state's income were one standard deviation above the mean, a TEL would increase spending by $427, about 16 percent. As Shadbegian (1996) points out, one interpretation of these results is that TELs may provide political cover for state policymakers. Legislators can claim that the government spending is not excessive because a TEL law designed specifically to set boundaries is in force. In effect, under some conditions (high state income) the TEL guidelines may become a floor for spending increases rather than a ceiling. Finally, the estimated coefficient for the Budget Cycle variable is only significant in the two-stage model in table 8.2. That estimate indicates that spending per capita is $95 more in biennial budgeting states relative to annual budgeting states, a 3 percent difference at the mean. This finding coincides with that in Kearns 1994. In the other models, the Budget Cycle variable is not significant at standard levels of confidence. Moreover, as will be discussed in additional detail, the length of the budget cycle appears to have a significant impact on spending volatility and thus an indirect effect on spending levels.

Effects of Fiscal Institutions on Revenues and Taxes

An often-voiced concern over a balanced budget requirement is its potential to force tax increases in response to a fiscal imbalance. Deficits will be eliminated by generating new revenues rather than by cutting spending. To examine this possibility, equation (8.3) is estimated first using total state revenues as the dependent variable and then using total tax revenues as the dependent variable.[10] These variables are again denominated both as a share of state income and per capita. Table 8.4 presents the results for Total Revenues, and table 8.5 presents the results for Total Taxes. These tables again report the results from using both the single-stage FGLS estimations and the two-stage techniques. Again, because of the endogeneity problem the two-stage estimates should be considered more reliable than the single-stage estimates.

Based on the endogenous models, a strict balanced budget requirement has no significant effect on per capita revenues or revenues as a share of income (table 8.4). In the tax revenue models (table 8.5), per capita taxes and taxes as a share of income appear to be significantly lower in states with a strict balanced budget requirement versus the other states. Recall that the comparable results in tables 8.2 and 8.3 indicate that a strict balanced budget requirement tends to constrain spending. Taken together, these results suggest that strict budget balance rules influence fiscal policy largely through expenditure adjustments and not through increases in taxes or other revenue sources. Concerning the results for the other institutional variables in tables 8.4 and 8.5, the most important feature is the similarity of their impact on revenues, taxes, and spending. The main exception is that the Budget Cycle variable shows a consistently negative, although somewhat small, correlation with state tax revenues.

Effects of Institutions on Fiscal Volatility

The findings in tables 8.2 and 8.3 regarding fiscal volatility introduce a novel dimension to the study of fiscal institutions. If institutions affect fiscal volatility, this establishes an indirect link to the size of government in addition to the direct link that has motivated previous studies of fiscal institutions. In essence, institutions such as the strict balanced budget requirement constrain spending to hold deficits in check (the direct link), but they may also add predictability to the level of spending from year to year. In turn, the predictability of state

TABLE 8.4.   Effects of Fiscal Institutions on State Government Revenues

Independent Variables	Dependent Variables = Revenues per Capita[a]		Dependent Variables = Revenues as a Share of Income	
	FGLS	Two-Stage	FGLS	Two-Stage
Expenditure Volatility	2.78	7.28	2.93	7.44
	(19.05)**	(18.65)**	(20.84)**	(22.58)**
Strict Balanced Budget	−196	17	−0.006	0.001
Requirement (= 1 if yes)	(−8.49)**	(0.63)	(−5.39)**	(0.65)
Item Reduction Veto Power	−342	−467	−0.015	−0.016
(= 1 if yes)	(−16.44)**	(−15.07)**	(−15.71)**	(−13.37)**
Supermaj. Required for Tax	−233	−129	−0.010	−0.012
Increase (= 1 if yes)	(−8.62)**	(−5.84)**	(−7.34)**	(−11.81)**
Tax or Expenditure Limitation	−1217	−774	−0.052	−0.032
(TEL) (= 1 if yes)	(−9.76)**	(−6.19)**	(−9.39)**	(−5.68)**
Interaction Term: TEL ×	0.060	0.045	0.000002	0.000002
Income per Capita	(10.73)**	(8.08)**	(10.34)**	(7.13)**
Biennial Budget Cycle	40	143	−0.0002	−0.0003
(= 1 if yes)	(2.35)*	(7.78)**	(−0.20)	(−.38)
Year dummy variables	Yes	Yes	Yes	Yes
Other variables included, see				
table 8.1	Model 2	Model 2	Model 1	Model 1
Wald chi-squared	9310**	8701**	4223**	4251**
Total panel observations[b]	1,363	1,363	1,363	1,363

Note Parameters are estimated using cross-sectional time-series FGLS regressions. z-statistics are shown in parentheses.

[a]Denominated in real (2000) dollars.

[b]Sample includes 47 states for the years 1970–98. Alaska, Hawaii, and Wyoming are omitted.

* Indicates significance at the 5 percent level for a two-tailed test. ** Indicates significance at the 1 percent level for a two-tailed test.

budgets reduces outlays because of this efficiency effect (the indirect link).

Equation (8.4) shows the form of the model used to investigate this indirect link:

$$\text{Expenditure Volatility}_i = \beta P_{it} + \gamma \text{Tax Volatility}_i$$
$$+ \Psi \text{Lame Duck}_i + \Phi \text{YPC}_{it}$$
$$+ \kappa \text{POP}_{it} + \alpha + \varepsilon_{it}. \tag{8.4}$$

Following the previous methodology the two measures of Expenditure Volatility described earlier are examined as dependent variables, one based on the volatility in expenditures per capita, and the other based on the volatility in expenditures as a share of income. The vector of institutional variables in P includes the same five variables described for equation (8.3). Equation (8.4) introduces two

TABLE 8.5.   Effects of Fiscal Institutions on State Tax Revenues

Independent Variables	Dependent Variable = Taxes per Capita[a]		Dependent Variable = Taxes as a Share of Income	
	FGLS	Two-Stage	FGLS	Two-Stage
Expenditure Volatility	−0.007	1.67	0.217	1.54
	(−0.11)	(9.59)**	(3.14)**	(9.97)**
Strict Balanced Budget	−87	−29	−0.004	−0.002
Requirement (= 1 if yes)	(−8.68)**	(−2.33)*	(−8.28)**	(−3.43)*
Item Reduction Veto Power	−147	−206	−0.007	−0.008
(= 1 if yes)	(−15.01)**	(−18.60)**	(−16.51)**	(−18.79)**
Supermaj. Required for Tax	−119	−114	−0.005	−0.006
Increase (= 1 if yes)	(−9.28)**	(−9.08)**	(−8.85)**	(−10.01)**
Tax or Expenditure Limitation	−757	−663	−0.034	−0.030
(TEL) (= 1 if yes)	(−11.23)**	(−9.70)**	(−11.07)**	(−9.57)**
Interaction Term: TEL × Income	0.031	0.029	0.000001	0.000001
per Capita	(10.77)**	(10.12)**	(10.69)**	(9.79)**
Biennial Budget Cycle (= 1 if yes)	−54	−27	−0.002	−0.003
	(−6.41)**	(−3.10)**	(−6.54)**	(−7.14)**
Year dummy variables	Yes	Yes	Yes	Yes
Other variables included, see				
table 8.1	Model 2	Model 3	Model 1	Model 1
Wald chi-squared	4944**	4921**	1105**	1184**
Total panel observations[b]	1,363	1,363	1,363	1,363

Note: Parameters are estimated using cross-sectional time-series FGLS regressions. z-statistics are shown in parentheses.

[a]Denominated in real (2000) dollars.

[b]Sample includes 47 states for the years 1970–98. Alaska, Hawaii, and Wyoming are omitted.

* Indicates significance at the 5 percent level for a two-tailed test. ** Indicates significance at the 1 percent level for a two-tailed test.

new variables into the analysis, the same variables used to identify the first-stage models in the two-stage estimations discussed previously. The Tax Volatility variable uses the values reflecting total taxes that were derived and presented in chapter 6. The Lame Duck variable measures the number of years in which a governor who was ineligible for reelection served (because of term limitation rules), as a share of the total years in the sample.[11] The expected relevance of this variable follows from the study by Besley and Case (1995b). They find higher state taxes and spending in years in which a governor could not seek reelection compared to years in which reelection to another term was possible. In other words, Besley and Case find that term limitations create state fiscal cycles. The cyclical fluctuations should be reflected in the Expenditure Volatility measures examined in equation (8.4). Finally, equation (8.4) includes two control variables, real income per capita (YPC) and population (POP). α is a constant term (state fixed effects are inappropriate), and ε is the regression error term.

Table 8.6 presents the results. Based on the per capita model, a TEL lowers volatility by $28 per capita, or about 17 percent in relation to the mean level of Expenditure Volatility (= $28/$162). A Strict Balanced Budget Requirement cuts spending volatility by 14 percent (= $22/$162). The results for the Item Reduction Veto indicate that this institution significantly amplifies spending volatility. Using the parameters in the per capita model, the Item Reduction Veto increases per capita spending volatility by 26 percent at the mean (= $42/$162). The results for the Supermajority Voting Requirement variable indicate a 4 percent reduction in the volatility of spending per capita (= $6/$162). A Biennial Budget cycle dampens Expenditure per Capita volatility by 12 percent (= $20/$162). (The coefficient on this variable is also negative but insignificant in the expenditure as a share of income model.)

The estimates in table 8.6 show a positive and significant relationship between the volatility in tax revenues and the volatility in spending. Again using the estimate in the per capita model, a one standard deviation increase in tax revenue volatility (= 0.001) increases per capita spending volatility by $23 (= 0.001 × 21408), or 14 percent in relation to the mean (= $23/$162). Using these point estimates as a rough indication of the elasticity, a 1 percent increase in tax revenue volatility translates into a 0.4 percent increase in spending volatility.

Finally, the coefficient on the Lame Duck variable is positive and significant in both models. Based on the per capita model, a one standard deviation increase in the share of Lame Duck years (= 0.29) increases per capita spending volatility by about \$5 (= 28 × 0.17), a 3 percent increase in relation to the mean (= \$5/\$162).

Commentary

This chapter exposits a straightforward theme: uncertainty is the enemy of efficiency in public as well as private enterprise. Budget volatility precludes efficient planning and adds significantly to the cost of government-provided services. Put differently, a reduction in spending volatility would be equivalent to a funding increase. The empirical evidence indicates that a 10 percent reduction in budget

TABLE 8.6.   **Effects of Institutions and Tax Revenue Volatility on State Spending Volatility**

Independent Variables	Dependent Variable = Volatility in Expenditures per Capita[a]	Dependent Variable = Volatility in Expenditures as a Share of Income[a]
Strict Balanced Budget Requirement	−22	−0.0008
(= 1 if yes)	(−5.32)**	(−3.70)**
Item Reduction Veto Power	42	0.0013
(= 1 if yes)	(7.89)**	(6.07)**
Supermaj. Required for Tax Increase	−6	0.0008
(= 1 if yes)	(−2.09)*	(5.02)**
Tax or Expenditure Limitation	−28	−0.0012
(TEL) (= 1 if yes)	(−8.87)**	(−7.95)**
Biennial Budget Cycle (= 1 if yes)	−20	−0.0001
	(−6.14)**	(−0.72)
Lame Duck Governor (% of years	0.17	0.00005
in sample)	(2.95)**	(1.98)*
Tax Revenue Volatility[b]	21408	1.18
	(12.10)**	(16.22)**
Income per Capita	0.004	0.0000
	(13.31)**	(1.11)
ln (Population)	−26	−0.001
	(−16.05)**	(−12.73)**
Constant	393	0.020
	(15.20)**	(13.59)**
R-squared	0.40	0.38
F-statistic	149**	105**
Total observations[c]	1,363	1,363

Note: Parameters are estimated using robust standard errors. *t*-statistics are shown in parentheses.

[a]Expenditure Volatility is measured as the standard deviation in the regression residuals from the core model in equation (8.1).

[b]See the derivation of the Tax Revenue Volatility variable in chapter 6.

[c]Alaska, Hawaii, and Wyoming are omitted.

* Indicates significance at the 5 percent level for a two-tailed test. ** Indicates significance at the 1 percent level for a two-tailed test.

volatility generates efficiency gains comparable to a 3.5 percent increase in the level of funding.

The trade-off between volatility and efficiency means that the role of fiscal institutions is more complex than previous analysis has generally assumed. Some institutions carry a dual role, exerting not only a direct influence on spending but also an indirect influence on the size of state budgets via their impact on fiscal stability. Consider for example a Strict Balanced Budget Requirement. The results in table 8.2 indicate that this institution cuts per capita spending directly by 3 percent. In addition, a Strict Balanced Budget Requirement dampens spending volatility by 14 percent (based on the estimates shown in table 8.6). This 14 percent reduction in spending volatility in turn leads to an additional 5 percent reduction in per capita spending. In essence, a Strict Balanced Budget Requirement lowers state spending by a combined 8 percent through these two channels.

Consideration of the indirect effects on fiscal institutions is particularly important in the analysis of TELs. The results in this chapter and those in prior studies (e.g., Shadbegian 1996) suggest that the direct effect of TELs diminishes in high income or rapidly growing states. But TELs contribute noticeably to budget stability, reducing spending volatility by 17 percent on average. Through that indirect channel TELs predictably reduce per capita spending by roughly 6 percent.

The analysis suggests that the reliability of tax revenues influences the size of government. Greater instability in tax revenues contributes to spending instability that impedes the efficiency of long-run state government operations. With less efficient planning, the level of government spending increases, which of course requires additional revenues.

In his 1997 comprehensive survey of the studies of state budget institutions James Poterba concludes that, while the evidence is not conclusive, the preponderance of studies suggests that institutions are not simply veils pierced by voters but important constraints on the nature of political bargaining. In essence, the demand for public spending is mediated through a set of fiscal and budget rules. The results in this chapter add fuel to Poterba's assessment that "fiscal institutions matter." With a new emphasis on fiscal volatility, institutions appear to matter more than past research has appreciated.

This goes beyond the fiscal rules assessed explicitly in this chapter such as the length of the budget cycle and tax and expenditure limitations. For example, Gilligan and Krehbeil (1989) develop a theoretical framework to assess the relationship between alternative legislative structures and policy uncertainty. They conclude that legislatures with radically majoritarian structures—those that permit very little power delegation or agenda control to specialists in committees—generate wider policy variations than legislatures that delegate control to specialized committees. Their analysis also implies that the choice of legislative procedures (e.g., the use of open versus closed rules for amending policies proposed by committees) may depend on the uncertainty of the policy environment. In other words, a host of alternative legislative and constitutional arrangements are likely to be interconnected with policy volatility, and the findings in this chapter stress the importance of studying these relationships in further detail.

Appendix

TABLE 8.AI.   Summary Statistics and Data Sources

Variable	Mean	Median	Standard Deviation
Expenditure per Capita[a]	$2,724	$2,648	$722
Expenditure/State Personal Income[b]	12.5%	12.3%	2.5%
Revenue per Capita[a]	$2,958	$2,865	$841
Revenue/State Personal Income[b]	13.5%	13.3%	2.9%
Total Taxes per Capita[a]	$1,178	$1,134	$332
Total Taxes/State Personal Income[b]	5.4%	5.4%	1.1%
Expenditure Volatility (Exp. per Capita)	$162	$149	$68
Expenditure Volatility (Exp./Income)	0.7%	0.6%	0.3%
Tax Revenue Volatility (Tax Rev./ Income)	0.3%	0.3%	0.1%
Lame Duck Governor (% of years)[c]	26%	20%	28%
Income per Capita[a]	$21,983	$21,512	$4,252
Unemployment Rate[d]	6.2%	5.9%	2.1%
ln (Population)[b]	15.0	15.1	1.0
Urban Population (% of population)[b]	65%	67%	22%
Population Age 18 to 64 (% of population)[b]	60%	60%	3%

[a]Denominated in real (2000) dollars. Data from U.S. Bureau of the Census Web Site.
[b]Data from U.S. Bureau of the Census Web Site.
[c]Data from Council of State Governments (Biennial Editions, 1968 through 2000), Duncan and Lawrence (Biennial Editions, 1968 through 2000), Barone and Sujifusa (Biennial Editions, 1968 through 2000), and correspondence with state election officials.
[d]Data from U.S. Bureau of Labor Statistics Web Site.

Chapter 9

Political Ideology and Other Drivers
of State Budget Priorities

State government budgets consist of four major spending categories: education; public welfare, health, and hospitals; highways; and police protection and corrections.[1] Combined, these four broad categories account for more than 70 percent of all state government spending. At the end of the twentieth century, for every budgetary dollar spent in the typical (median) state, 33¢ went for education; 27¢ went for public welfare, health, and hospitals; 8¢ went for highways; and 4¢ went for police protection and corrections. Naturally, these expenditure allocations mirror the key responsibilities and functions of American state governments. For emphasis, figure 9.1 illustrates the budgetary pie sliced into these four components for the typical state government in 1998.

In the final three decades of the twentieth century the relative importance of these four components shifted, and for two components the budget reallocation was striking. Figure 9.2 illustrates the budget slices in the typical state in 1969. Most noteworthy, over this 30-year period the share of the budget allocated to highway programs dropped 11 percentage points. The drop in highway spending was almost exactly offset by a 10 percentage point rise in spending for public welfare, health, and hospitals. In 30 years, state highway expenditures dropped from the second largest budget item (19 percent in 1969) to a distant third, amounting to just 8 percent of the typical state budget in 1998. At the same time, spending for public welfare, health, and hospitals rose from third place (17 percent in 1969) to a strong second place, amounting to 27 percent of the typical state budget in 1998. The reallocation from highways to public welfare and health-related programs represents by far the most conspicuous transformation in state budgetary priorities in the late twentieth century.

Education spending remained the largest budget component throughout this three-decade period, but its share of the budget dropped 4 percentage points in the typical state, from 37 percent to

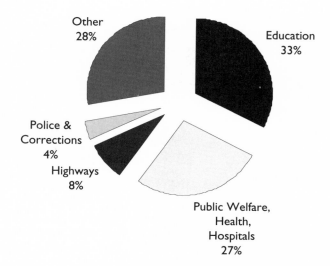

Fig. 9.1. Major components of state budgets in 1998 (values for the median state)

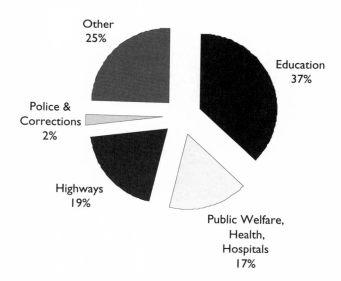

Fig. 9.2. Major components of state budgets in 1969 (values for the median state)

33 percent. Police protection and corrections spending increased 2 percentage points, from 2 percent to 4 percent. The "other" category increased 3 percentage points, to 28 percent from 25 percent.

This broad blueprint of the relative importance the major spending programs in the typical (median) state fails to capture the rich diversity among the states in budget priorities. For example, Utah devotes 43 percent of its state budget to funding education; in Massachusetts and New Hampshire only 20 percent of the state budget goes to education. New York devotes 39 percent of its budget to public welfare, health and hospitals; Alaska devotes 16 percent.

In addition, states differ widely in how their budget priorities changed over the 30 years examined. In Florida education spending as a share of the state budget fell 20 percentage points; in Idaho education spending rose by 5 percentage points. It is interesting to note that highway funding as a share of the budget fell in all 50 states between 1969 and 1998, with the greatest decline in Wyoming (20 percentage points) and the smallest decline in Massachusetts (2 percentage points).

Basic Trends in State Budget Priorities

Chapter 7 documented the changes that occurred over 30 years in aggregate state spending, and Chapter 8 identified the main elements that account for spending differences over time and across states. In per capita terms, total spending in the median state grew from $1,696 per capita in 1969 to $3,593 in 1998 (in constant 2000 dollars). This growth amounts to an average annual growth rate of 2.6 percent. By comparison, between 1969 and 1998 personal income per capita in the median state grew at an average annual rate of 1.7 percent. Figure 9.3 shows the comparable growth rates for the four main budget components between 1969 and 1998.

Real per capita spending for police protection and corrections grew at an annual rate of 5.2 percent, exactly twice the growth rate in aggregate state spending. Public welfare, health, and hospitals spending grew at an average annual clip of 4.2 percent, again well above the growth rate in aggregate state spending. Education spending per capita grew at a 2 percent annual rate, slower than the aggregate budget growth yet still faster than the 1.7 percent growth in state personal income. Perhaps the most surprising result pertains to state highway spending; it declined at an average annual rate of 0.4 percent. In 1998, highway spending in the median state equaled $276 per capita, down from $310 per capita in 1969 (both denominated in 2000 dollars).

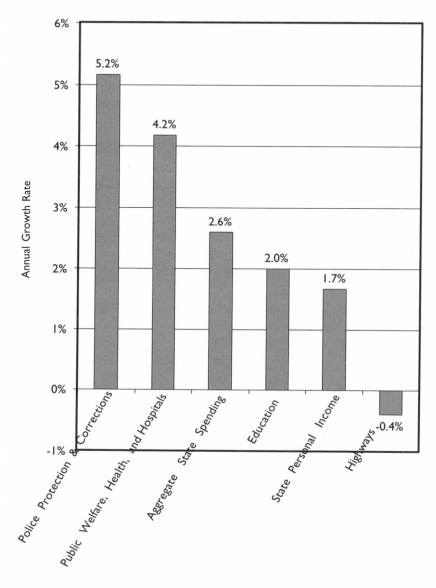

Fig. 9.3. Comparative growth in major budget components, 1969–98 (values reflect the annual growth rate in real per capita spending)

Convergence in State Budget Components

The aggregate level of state spending exhibited little convergence after the mid-1970s, as chapter 7 explored in considerable detail. For example, the dispersion across states in aggregate spending as a share of income in 1998 equaled its value in 1977 (see fig. 7.8). Likewise, figure 7.7 shows that much of the convergence in spending per capita occurred in the early 1970s and that the dispersion in aggregate per capita spending remained almost flat for 20 years, from 1975 until 1994.

Here we investigate convergence in the four major budget components. A convergence pattern would suggest an underlying process in which states with below-average spending tend to catch up with neighboring states. For example, below-average education spending might become the subject of heated political discussion, with candidates for state offices pledging to increase funding to the "national average." This process is sometimes labeled "benchmarking," as candidates and voters use information about funding levels in other states to gauge their own state's performance (see Besley and Case 1995a).

The basic method used in chapter 7 to measure convergence is reemployed here. Convergence is again measured by the coefficient of variation in spending for a specific component across the states in a given year.[2] These yearly values for each budget category are computed for the period 1969 through 1998. Spending for each budget component is denominated and displayed in three ways. Figure 9.4 plots the coefficient of variation using the natural log of spending per capita. Figure 9.5 plots the pattern using spending as a share of state income, and figure 9.6 uses spending as a share of the total state budget.

In figure 9.4 (which uses per capita spending) the police protection and corrections component shows a clear convergence trend, with the coefficient of variation dropping 42 percent over the three decades. Likewise, public welfare, health, and hospitals spending and education spending exhibit convergence, although the trend is much less pronounced than for police protection and corrections. The pattern for highway spending is less clear, and in fact the coefficient of variation in 1998 is 15 percent higher than it was in 1969.

The broad patterns in figure 9.5 (based on spending as a share of state income) are quite similar to those in figure 9.4. The police protection and corrections component exhibits the sharpest convergence; public welfare, health, and hospitals spending and education

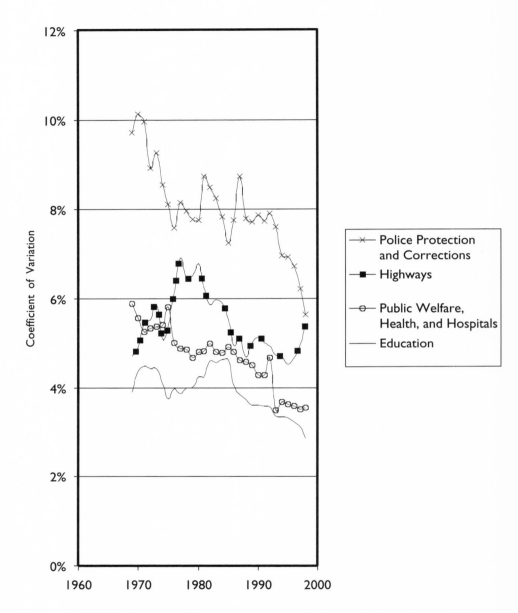

Fig. 9.4.   Convergence/divergence among states in budget priorities (spending per capita)

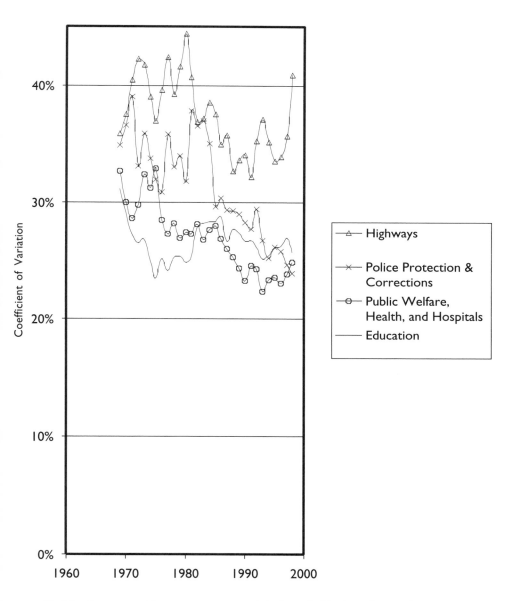

Fig. 9.5.   Convergence/divergence among states in budget priorities (spending as a share of income)

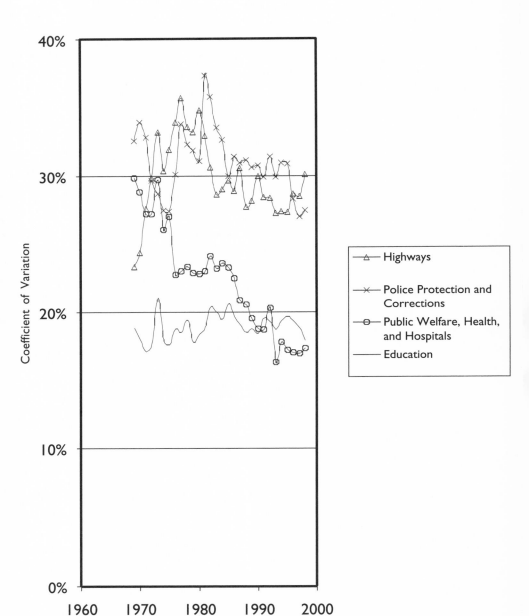

Fig. 9.6.   Convergence/divergence among states in budget priorities (spending as a share of total state budget)

spending exhibit modest convergence, and highway spending shows no secular tendency either way. The patterns in figure 9.6 (based on spending as a share of the total budget) differ somewhat from the two prior measures. The education component and the highway component show no signs of convergence, whereas the sharpest convergence trend appears for the public welfare, health, and hospitals component. Police protection and corrections spending as a share of the budget shows no convergence since the mid-1970s, the same pattern we observed for aggregate state spending.

With the possible exception of spending for welfare, health, and hospitals, the disparity among states in specific types of spending does not seem to be driven by a simple convergence process. This coincides with the central interpretation of the data for overall state spending. We next investigate a host of factors that potentially determine the composition of state budgets.

What Determines State Budget Priorities?

The investigation of spending for specific budget components follows the empirical procedure laid out in chapter 8. The first step estimates for each of the four spending categories a core regression model that controls for standard economic and demographic features in a state in a given year. The second step computes the metric for spending volatility for each budget category and reestimates the model by adding the volatility measure and the fiscal institutional variables. The key extension here is to bring political ideology explicitly into the analysis.

The introduction of political ideology variables seeks to capture the influence of "tastes," or policy preferences, that stand apart from the influence of specific economic interests. For example, high unemployment rates, low per capita incomes, and a large elderly population should proxy the extent of potential beneficiaries from public health and welfare programs. These direct beneficiaries might reasonably favor such programs on self-interest grounds. However, other voters and policymakers might support health and welfare programs purely on ideological grounds. The importance of ideological support for particular programs would not necessarily be picked up in the economic and demographic control variables.

To examine the influence of ideologically determined policy preferences the models include two measures of political ideology, one for state citizens and one for state political leaders.[3] These two ideology indices are constructed to reflect political orientation along a liberal-conservative continuum, with 0 indicating the most conservative position and 100 the most liberal position.

Table 9.1 reports the two indices for the most recently available years. Based on the Citizen Ideology index, the ten most liberal states are Massachusetts, Hawaii, Maine, New York, Rhode Island, Connecticut, New Jersey, Maryland, West Virginia, and Illinois. The ten most conservative states are Oklahoma, Idaho, Nebraska, Mississippi, Arizona, Utah, Montana, Alabama, Wyoming, and Louisiana. The indices further indicate that the political ideology within some states changed substantially between 1970 and 1997. Based on the percentage change in the Citizen Ideology index, the largest shifts toward liberalism occurred in South Carolina, Georgia, Virginia, North Carolina, and Alabama. The largest shifts toward conservatism occurred in Idaho, Oklahoma, Alaska, Montana, and Utah. Between 1970 and 1997, 25 states became more conservative, 24 states became more liberal, and California remained unchanged. The analysis explores the responsiveness of budgetary priorities to these indicators of political ideology.

Factors that Influence State Budget Allocations

Table 9.2 presents the results for the core model containing the economic and demographic variables for each budget component.[4] The core models for education; public welfare, health, and hospitals; and highways are estimated with a high degree of precision, while the "within-state" R-squared of 0.37 for the highways model is more modest. The two economic factors in the models, per capita income and the unemployment rate, exert prominent effects on each budget component except education spending. In that model neither income nor unemployment is statistically significant. An increase in the unemployment rate tends to increase spending on public welfare and police protection and to detract from spending on highways. Spending in all three of these categories is boosted by increases in state income.

Consistent with the findings for total spending described in chapter 8, we find evidence of economies of scale in per capita spending on education, public welfare, and highways. That is, per capita spending falls as state population increases. In contrast, per capita spending for police protection and corrections rises with population, evidence of diseconomies of scale. We find a mixed bag of results with respect to the percentage of the population in urban areas; in urban areas per capita

TABLE 9.1. Political Ideology Ratings

	Citizen Index, 1997	Citizen % Change	Government Index, 1996	Government % Change
Alabama	36	12	31	35
Alaska	28	−61	41	−36
Arizona	25	−38	2	−88
Arkansas	45	89	69	206
California	54	0	30	−3
Colorado	46	20	56	343
Connecticut	68	15	43	−42
Delaware	43	−9	64	163
Florida	44	78	62	187
Georgia	42	250	77	386
Hawaii	74	−10	94	1
Idaho	14	−73	2	−90
Illinois	60	23	17	−30
Indiana	40	−15	44	446
Iowa	41	−22	24	19
Kansas	44	24	10	−73
Kentucky	34	−11	69	82
Louisiana	30	52	39	61
Maine	72	17	63	−17
Maryland	62	10	90	77
Massachusetts	83	14	70	−2
Michigan	57	−5	16	−70
Minnesota	56	−3	43	11
Mississippi	24	109	26	117
Missouri	44	1	69	6
Montana	27	−45	3	−96
Nebraska	21	−25	74	1200
Nevada	33	13	51	168
New Hampshire	40	−9	1	−94
New Jersey	67	1	34	−14
New Mexico	43	1	52	23
New York	69	1	44	−10
North Carolina	42	154	60	128
North Dakota	48	−1	7	−86
Ohio	48	−6	15	−38
Oklahoma	8	−73	11	−61
Oregon	54	3	59	9
Pennsylvania	58	−2	25	−43
Rhode Island	69	−13	62	−30
South Carolina	41	272	25	44
South Dakota	42	−15	7	9
Tennessee	35	25	24	−38
Texas	40	48	31	−20
Utah	27	−44	5	−65
Vermont	59	−2	84	75
Virginia	42	248	26	111
Washington	51	−12	61	83
West Virginia	60	14	81	61
Wisconsin	52	−9	28	17
Wyoming	30	−21	7	74

Note: Data from William D. Berry et al. 1998. A value of 0 indicates the most conservative position and 100 the most liberal position. The Citizen % Change for the Citizen index is for 1970 to 1997, and the Government % Change for the Government index is for 1970 to 1996.

spending rises for education and highways and falls for public welfare and police protection and corrections. As the percentage of the population between 18 and 64 rises we observe a rise in education spending and a decline in spending for highways and police protection and corrections. In the public welfare equation the coefficient controlling for population age is positive but statistically insignificant.

Importance of Expenditure Volatility and Fiscal Institutions on the Major Budget Components

Table 9.3 shows the findings for expenditure volatility and fiscal institutions for the four budget components.[5] The Expenditure Volatility variable exhibits a positive and significant correlation with education and public welfare spending (the two largest budget components) but not with highway or police protection and correction spending. Com-

TABLE 9.2. Major Budget Components: Regression Results for Core Models with Demographic and Economic Factors

| Independent Variables | Real per Capita Spending on[a] | | | |
	Education	Public Welfare, Health, & Hospitals	Highways	Police Protection & Corrections
Income per Capita[a]	−0.003	0.019	0.014	0.006
	(−1.35)	(7.90)**	(10.12)**	(14.40)**
Unemployment Rate	−3.84	6.90	−2.28	0.95
	(−1.95)	(3.37)**	(−1.98)*	(2.48)*
ln (Population)	−139	−260	−81	17
	(−4.96)**	(−8.90)**	(−4.95)**	(3.04)**
Urban Population (% of population)	5.08	−6.02	2.36	−1.94
	(3.07)**	(−3.50)**	(2.44)**	(−6.01)**
Population Age 18 to 64 (% of population)	7.44	5.88	−8.06	−2.91
	(2.24)*	(1.71)	(−4.16)**	(−4.84)**
State fixed effects	Yes	Yes	Yes	Yes
Year dummy variables	Yes	Yes	Yes	Yes
R-squared, within states	0.74	0.87	0.37	0.81
R-squared, between states	0.01	0.09	0.01	0.20
R-squared, overall	0.24	0.06	0.05	0.15
F-statistic	111**	268**	23**	168**
Total panel observations[b]	1,363	1,363	1,363	1,363

Note: Parameters are estimated using cross-sectional time-series FGLS regressions. z-statistics are shown in parentheses.

[a]Denominated in real (2000) dollars.

[b]Sample includes 47 states for the years 1970–98. Alaska, Hawaii, and Wyoming are omitted.

* Indicates significance at the 5 percent level for a two-tailed test. ** Indicates significance at the 1 percent level for a two-tailed test.

puting the respective elasticities allows us to compare the magnitudes of these volatility effects. Table 9.4 reports these elasticities for the budget components, as well as for the elasticity of total spending with respect to volatility, which equals 0.35 (as computed in chapter 8). As shown in table 9.4, a 1 percent increase in volatility amounts to a 0.4 percent increase in public welfare spending and a 0.33 percent increase in education spending. In other words, this suggests that the efficiency of public welfare programs is more sensitive to planning uncertainty than the typical program in the state budget. The efficiency of education spending appears to be slightly less sensitive to uncertainty than the typical budget program.

TABLE 9.3. Major Budget Components: Regression Results for Expenditure Volatility and Fiscal Institutions

Independent Variables	Real per Capita Spending on[a]			
	Education	Public Welfare, Health, & Hospitals	Highways	Police Protection & Corrections
Expenditure Volatility of Budget	4.61	2.51	0.51	−0.36
Component	(11.40)**	(4.71)**	(1.91)	(−0.90)
Strict Balanced Budget	87	−87	15	−5
Requirement (= 1 if yes)	(7.09)**	(−5.69)**	(3.99)**	(−2.67)**
Item Reduction Veto Power	−170	72	20	−15
(= 1 if yes)	(−19.99)**	(4.27)**	(5.65)**	(−9.70)**
Supermaj. Required for Tax	−74	36	−2	5
Increase (= 1 if yes)	(−6.74)**	(2.23)*	(−0.41)	(3.72)**
Tax or Expenditure Limitation	−213	−455	7	−32
(TEL) (= 1 if yes)	(−3.62)**	(−9.25)**	(0.36)	(−4.37)**
Interaction Term: TEL × Income	0.008	0.018	−0.0004	0.002
per Capita	(3.08)**	(8.43)**	(−0.52)	(6.13)**
Biennial Budget Cycle (= 1 if yes)	6	20	17	−8
	(0.87)	(2.10)*	(5.88)**	(−7.69)**
Year dummy variables	Yes	Yes	Yes	Yes
Other variables included, see				
tables 9.1 and 9.6	Column 1	Column 2	Column 3	Column 4
Wald chi-squared	2651**	6898**	3168**	5609**
Total panel observations[b]	1,316	1,316	1,316	1,316

Note: Parameters are estimated using cross-sectional time-series FGLS regressions. z-statistics are shown in parentheses.

[a]Denominated in real (2000) dollars.

[b]Sample includes 47 states: Alaska, Hawaii, and Wyoming are omitted. The sample period is 1970–97, the last year for which the Citizen Ideology index data are available.

[c]The models reported control for the Citizen Ideology index. The results for this variable are reported in table 9.6.

* Indicates significance at the 5 percent level for a two-tailed test. ** Indicates significance at the 1 percent level for a two-tailed test.

Table 9.5 further illustrates and compares the impact of budget volatility on outlays for the major spending categories. There the elasticity estimates from table 9.4 are used to assess the consequences of a 1 percent increase in budget volatility on per capita spending for each budget category. These estimated effects on outlays are evaluated at the respective sample means. For example, consider the results for education spending. As shown in table 9.4, a 1 percent increase in education expenditure volatility yields a 0.33 percent increase in education spending per capita. As table 9.5 reports, this increase would equal $30 per capita based on the sample mean for education spending. For public welfare spending, a 1 percent increase in budget volatility results in a 0.40 percent spending increase, or $26 per capita, as shown in table 9.5. The estimated coefficient for expenditure volatility is not significant in either the highways or the police protection and

TABLE 9.4.   Relative Importance of Ideology versus Expenditure Volatility: Elasticity Estimates

	Education	Public Welfare, Health, & Hospitals	Highways	Police Protection & Corrections	Total Spending
Expenditure Volatility of Budget Component	**0.33**	**0.40**	0.06	−0.03	**0.35**
Citizen Ideology index	**−0.04**	**0.20**	−0.08	−0.14	**0.17**
Government Ideology index	0.001	**0.10**	−0.04	−0.01	**−0.07**

Note: The values in the table reflect point elasticity estimates computed at the sample means for the respective budget components. Values in bold type indicate that the relationship is statistically significant at the 5 percent or the 1 percent level of confidence.

TABLE 9.5.   Relative Importance of Ideology versus Expenditure Volatility: Impact on per Capita Spending of a 1 Percent Increase (in $)

	Education	Public Welfare, Health, & Hospitals	Highways	Police Protection & Corrections	Total Spending
Expenditure Volatility of Budget Component	**30**	**26**	2	−0.30	**95**
Citizen Ideology index	**−3**	**13**	−2	−1	**47**
Government Ideology index	0.10	**6**	−1	−0.05	**19**

Note: These dollar estimates use the elasticities shown in table 9.4 and evaluate the impact at the sample means for each budget component. Values in bold type indicate that the relationship is statistically significant at the 5 percent or the 1 percent level of confidence.

corrections models, and the estimated size of the volatility effect is likewise miniscule for these two budget components.

In summary, uncertainty about future funding levels has considerable impact on the two largest programs in state budgets: education and public welfare. This finding suggests that reductions in uncertainty that facilitate efficient operating techniques in these critical functions of state government would yield potentially large savings for taxpayers.

The models shown in table 9.3 reveal stark differences with respect to how fiscal institutions affect specific spending categories. The item reduction veto power appears to have a major impact on curtailing education spending and only minor consequences for police protection and corrections spending. Tax and expenditure limitations have a large effect on welfare-related spending and no effect at all on highway spending. A supermajority requirement for a tax increase restrains spending for education-related programs but not spending for welfare-related programs. In essence, these findings suggest that fiscal institutions have consequences that go well beyond the overall size of state budgets. Not all budget categories are affected equally, and thus institutions appear to influence the allocation of spending among major programs.

Political Ideology Matters

The models assess the impact of political ideology on state spending decisions while taking into account economic, demographic, and institutional factors. The relevant regression coefficients and test statistics are reported in table 9.6, the elasticities are reported in table 9.4, and the projected impact of a 1 percent change in political ideology is reported in table 9.5.[6] The index for Citizen Ideology has a statistically significant coefficient in all four models, and the index for Government Ideology has a statistically significant coefficient in the models for public welfare and highways (see table 9.6).

Political ideology plays the greatest role in determining public welfare, health, and hospitals spending. A 1 percent increase in Citizen Ideology (the degree of liberalism increases by 1 percent) results in a 0.20 percent spending increase in welfare-related programs. Evaluated at the sample mean, this ideology shift would expand welfare funding by $13 per capita. Government ideology also significantly affects welfare funding, and the estimated elasticity is 0.10. At the state mean, this implies that a 1 percent rise in Government

Ideology (a shift toward liberalism) is associated with a $6 per capita rise in welfare funding.

Political ideology has the second largest impact on spending for police protection and corrections. For that component, a 1 percent shift in citizen liberalism amounts to a 0.14 percent decline in spending. The comparable effect of a more liberal citizenry is a 0.08 percent drop in highway funding and a 0.04 percent drop in education funding. The Government Ideology coefficient is negative and statistically significant for highway spending, but the estimated impact on spending is quite small. A 1 percent shift in government liberalism amounts to only about $1 per capita. Finally, the results for total state spending indicate that a 1 percent rise in citizen liberalism increases the mean state budget by $47 per capita. A 1 percent rise in government ideology increases the mean state budget by $19 per capita.

The impact of ideology on total state spending is shown graphically in figure 9.7, and the impact of ideology on the four budget components is graphed in figure 9.8. Both figures plot the relationships holding the other control variables constant at their sample mean values. Taken together, these results indicate that political ideology affects both the size of state budgets and how funds are allocated within the budget.

Consider states such as Arizona, Indiana, or Wisconsin, which have become relatively more conservative since 1970. The budgetary

TABLE 9.6. Major Budget Components: Regression Results for Citizen and Government Political Ideology Indices

	Real Per Capita Spending on[a]			
	Education	Public Welfare, Health, & Hospitals	Highways	Police Protection & Corrections
Citizen Ideology index[b]	−0.70	2.81	−0.51	−0.25
	(−2.64)**	(10.18)**	(−4.26)**	(−6.57)**
Government Ideology index[b]	−0.12	1.31	−0.21	−0.01
	(−0.70)	(9.45)**	(−3.14)**	(−0.42)
Other variables included, see tables 9.2 and 9.3	Column 1	Column 2	Column 3	Column 4

Note: Parameters are estimated using cross-sectional time-series FGLS regressions. z-statistics are shown in parentheses.

[a]Denominated in real (2000) dollars.

[b]Data for the Citizen Ideology index are available through 1997, and data for the Government Ideology index are available through 1996.

* Indicates significance at the 5 percent level for a two-tailed test. ** Indicates significance at the 1 percent level for a two-tailed test.

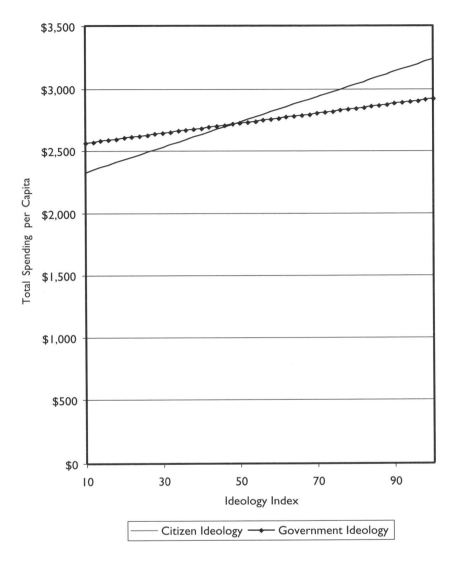

Fig. 9.7. Effect of citizen and government ideology on total spending (most liberal ideology = 100)

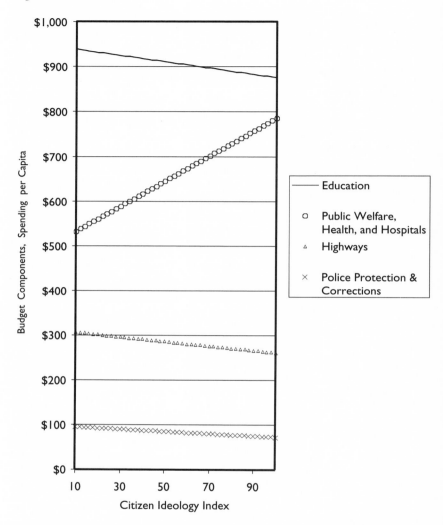

Fig. 9.8.   Effect of citizen ideology on budget priorities (most liberal ideology = 100)

implication of this ideological trend is to constrain overall state spending, with welfare, health, and hospitals spending taking a disproportionately large hit. This happens because, as the total budget shrinks, funding tends to increase slightly for education, highways, and police protection programs. Alternatively, consider a trend toward a more liberal citizenry, such as in Florida, North Carolina, or

Texas. The budgetary implication is an overall spending increase, with disproportionately large increases in welfare, health, and hospitals funding, at the expense of police protection and corrections, highway, and education funding.

Commentary

The late Aaron Wildavsky eloquently articulated the notion that government budgets reflect the underlying values and preferences of society: "Ask how budgets should be made and you will be asking how social life ought to be lived" (Webber and Wildavsky 1980, 22). This genre of a citizen or voter-oriented model of fiscal policy-making has a long tradition in political science. The analysis of state budgets in this chapter supports a voter-oriented framework to a substantial degree. Even after controlling for a barrage of economic, demographic, and institutional factors, political ideology significantly and independently affects the size and composition of state spending.

It is important to note that the analysis adds perspective regarding the relative influence of various forces. How much does political ideology influence budgetary outcomes? Political ideology appears to matter less than other factors such as fiscal stability and specific institutional arrangements. In short, models that treat state institutions as relatively transparent and neutral communicators of voter preferences have severely limited explanatory power.

Appendix

TABLE 9.A1.   Summary Statistics and Data Sources

Variable	Mean	Median	Standard Deviation
Education (Expenditure per Capita)[a]	$910	$885	$227
Public Welfare, Health, & Hospitals (Expenditure per Capita)[a]	$644	$576	$285
Highways (Expenditure per Capita)[a]	$287	$273	$94
Police Protection & Corrections (Expenditure per Capita)[a]	$85	$73	$43
Education Expenditure Volatility	$73	$67	$28
Public Welfare, Health, & Hospitals Expenditure Volatility	$75	$71	$30
Highways Expenditure Volatility	$40	$34	$21
Police Protection & Corrections Expenditure Volatility	$14	$12	$7
Citizen Ideology[b]	46	46	16
Government Ideology[b]	49	48	22

[a]Denominated in real (2000) dollars. Data from U.S. Bureau of the Census Web Site.
[b]Data from Berry et al. 1998.

Chapter 10

Fresh Perspectives on Familiar Problems

The interjection of the volatility dimension breathes new life into well-plowed fields of political economy. Start with the extensive diversity in living standards among the American states, diversity that increased even further in the closing decades of the twentieth century. This pattern of income divergence defies the convergence pattern anticipated by neoclassical growth theory. The mean-variance perspective finds fertile soil in this crevice between fact and theory. States not only differ widely with respect to living standards and growth, but they differ widely with respect to the volatility of their economies. The metrics constructed to assess and compare state economic volatility provide the means to unearth a new and fundamental relationship. State income and state volatility are positively correlated, analogous to the fundamental risk-return trade-off at the heart of modern portfolio theory.

High volatility tempers the attractiveness of high-income states to potential workers and investors, which implies that income differentials may persist when factor location decisions take into account these dual criteria. In the neoclassical framework, differentials among states in expected incomes and rates of return alone drive factor mobility. But that analysis overlooks an essential element of the market adjustment process. A stable state economy substitutes for a hike in income for the same reason that some investors prefer a low-risk, low-return portfolio to a high-risk, high-return portfolio. Put differently, higher than average state incomes appear to reflect in part a risk premium. Furthermore, low-income states experience commensurately low levels of economic volatility, a finding that confounds a simple judgment about state economic conditions. Risk-sensitive residents could reasonably judge state stability as an attribute of a successful economy. The mean-variance perspective at once helps to explain state economic diversity and makes more difficult the appraisal of state economic performance.

In the domain of fiscal policy, the focus on volatility exposes new ground. Consider the analysis of revenue volatility. Conventional theory and practice embraces the view that sales taxes generate a highly reliable revenue stream. This thesis holds that household consumption patterns vary less over time than household income and that this consumption-smoothing effect carries over to the revenues derived from these alternative tax bases. Yet, the appropriate measures of revenue reliability indicate otherwise. In almost two-thirds of the states that levy both individual income taxes and sales taxes, revenues from the sales tax are more volatile than revenues from the income tax. The conventional wisdom that the sales tax provides a relatively reliable revenue stream has no factual basis in the American states.

Similarly confounding conventional wisdom, the evidence strongly indicates that state economic performance is more sensitive to marginal rates in the sales tax than it is to marginal rates in the individual income tax. A number of prior studies have investigated the impact of taxes on state economic performance, but none has isolated and evaluated the separate effects of sales versus income taxes.

The evidence that sales taxes imperil state economic performance offers a plausible explanation for the growing aversion by most states to a heavy dependence on the sales tax. In the 1960s sales taxes were the predominant tax revenue source for American state governments, accounting for nearly 80 percent of tax revenues in the median state. By the end of the twentieth century sales taxes were roughly on a par with income taxes in the typical state. As the empirical findings subsequently indicate, volatile tax revenues beget spending volatility that fuels budget increases that, in turn, require additional revenue. Given that sales taxes offer little in the way of volatility relief and that they deter economic growth, state policymakers have clear incentives to steer away from this tax instrument.

The observations and analyses regarding state taxes convey a broad lesson of considerable importance. What might be sound tax policy for a large, national economy (the use of consumption taxes) does not translate into good policy for a small, open economy such as an American state. The theory that a consumption (sales) tax encourages savings and therefore growth-promoting investments makes little sense at the state level. The reason is twofold. First, even if a state's sales tax restrains consumption expenditures, the increased pool of savings flows readily across state lines. That is, any expansion in investment activity from the sales tax–induced savings can hardly be expected to remain within the borders of the state that levied the tax. Other states and nations reap the investment benefits from one state's tax inducement to save. Second, consumers residing in high-tax states make at least some of their purchases from vendors located in low- and no-tax states. Legally, a consumer who makes an out-of-state purchase is required to remit the applicable sales tax to his or her state of residence, but compliance with this essentially self-policed rule is minimal. Looking ahead, the adverse growth consequences of the sales tax exposed by analysis of late-twentieth-century data will be magnified greatly in an economy immersed in electronic transactions. The ubiquity of the Internet as a vehicle for electronic commerce undoubtedly will fuel an explosion in out-of-state purchases in the twenty-first century. For this reason we can anticipate an acceleration in the documented demise of the state sales tax.

The splurge in American state government spending in the final three decades of the twentieth century was perhaps overshadowed by concerns about the exploding national debt. Yet, in 1998 the size of the federal government as a proportion of national income sank below its level in 1969. Meanwhile, state government spending as a share of income continued to rise at an annual clip of about 1 percent in the typical state. Here again diversity is the rule, and the convergence thesis explains little about the pattern of spending among states.

The mean-variance perspective applied to state budget processes provides at least a partial explanation for state spending patterns. The historical analysis of state spending reveals that budget volatility is positively correlated with spending. This raises the important theme that fiscal uncertainty is the enemy of government efficiency. Within this context, the impact of state fiscal institutions takes on new relevance. Institutions such as balanced budget requirements, tax and expenditure limitations, biennial budgeting, and the item veto affect fiscal volatility and through this channel have indirect effects as well as direct effects on the size of government. The results of this analysis indicate that fiscal institutions play a more subtle and significant role in the state budgetary process than traditional analyses have appreciated.

The material role of fiscal volatility offers constructive suggestions for state policymakers. For instance, implementing procedures that promote budget stability significantly improves agency planning and efficiency, and such changes can improve state services without additional expenditures. In addition to the biennial budget process that was explicitly examined, other procedures such as funding programs via multiyear block grants would appear to offer comparable benefits.

In general, institutions that reduce the uncertainty in government agency planning yield potentially large gains in efficiency.

This study began with a familiar question: why do the American state economies grow at such vastly different rates and manifest wide differences in living standards? The elevated importance of economic and fiscal volatility offers new policy-relevant insights and ideas that map a course for future research.

Notes

Chapter 1

1. The values in figure 1.2 use the annual growth rate in real per capita incomes, continuously compounded. The formula is $[\ln(X_t/X_0)]/n$, where ln is the natural logarithm, X_t is the value at the end of the period, X_0 is the value at the beginning of the period, and n is the number of years.

2. The results in table 1.1 based on equation (1.1) use Newey-White standard errors with an AR(1) lag structure to correct for first-order serial correlation. Indicator (dummy) variables for the specific time periods interacted with the Trend$_t$ variable test for significant changes in the growth rates between time periods.

3. These 13 states are Alabama, Arkansas, Florida, Idaho, Kansas, Kentucky, Mississippi, New Mexico, Oklahoma, South Carolina, Tennessee, Virginia, and West Virginia.

4. These additional nine states are California, Georgia, Louisiana, Maryland, Minnesota, Missouri, North Carolina, Pennsylvania, and Wisconsin.

5. Canjels and Watson 1997 find that the least squares growth rate is more robust to differences in the serial correlation properties of the data than the geometric or continuously compounded rate of growth. See also Easterly and Rebelo 1993 for additional discussion in the context of comparing growth rates across nations. The least squares method computes the growth rate by regressing the natural logarithm of income in each state on a linear time trend, as shown in equations (1.2a) and (1.2b):

$$\ln (\text{Real Income per Capita}_t) = \text{Constant} + \beta_{ypc}$$
$$(\text{Time Trend}_{1969-99}) + u_t, \qquad (1.2a)$$

$$\ln (\text{Real Income per Worker}_t) = \text{Constant} + \beta_{ypw}$$
$$(\text{Time Trend}_{1969-99}) + u_t, \qquad (1.2b)$$

where ln refers to the natural logarithm, the subscript t refers to the value in each year, and u_t is the random error term. In this specification the estimated coefficients for β_{ypc} and β_{ypw} yield the annual growth rates. Equations (1.2a) and (1.2b) are estimated using Newey-White standard errors with an AR(1) lag structure to correct for first-order serial correlation. The robustness issue becomes particularly relevant for the procedures employed in chapter 2 to test for income convergence.

6. If two variables are perfectly correlated the simple correlation coefficient is 1. Two totally uncorrelated variables have a simple correlation coefficient of 0. The correlation in the state rankings based on the two methods of measuring growth is also 0.86.

7. To some extent the income per worker measure avoids an inherent weakness in the income per capita measure. For example, suppose individuals migrate out of a poorly performing state. This population exodus drives up income per capita in that state, even though its income did not improve. The income per worker metric comes a bit closer than the income per person metric to economists' standard concept of "productivity," which seeks to measure output per hour of labor.

Chapter 2

1. This sketch of the forces underlying state income convergence stresses the mobility of productive factors facilitated by open state borders. However, the fundamental implication in the neoclassical model that income levels will converge to a steady state does not require open borders and factor mobility. In a closed economy, income levels converge to a steady state because of diminishing returns to incremental capital investments. Factor mobility greatly reinforces the convergence phenomenon.

2. Much attention has been paid in the literature on economic growth to the phenomenon of "conditional convergence," the tendency of economies with lower-level incomes to grow faster, conditional on their rate of factor accumulation. Perhaps the most cited study supporting condition convergence using international data is Mankiw, Romer, and Weil 1992. However, Pritchett (1997) documents that, regardless of conditional convergence, perhaps *the* basic fact of modern economic history is massive absolute divergence in the distribution of incomes across countries. Pritchett estimates that between 1870 and 1985 the ratio of incomes in the richest and poorest countries increased sixfold, the standard deviation of (natural log) per capita incomes increased by between 60 and 100 percent, and the average income gap between the richest and poorest countries grew almost ninefold (from $1,500 to over $12,000).

3. The coefficient of variation is derived by dividing the standard deviation by the mean. Examining the dispersion in the logarithm of the level of per capita income, not the dispersion in the level itself, is the correct way to test for convergence in the growth rates. If the rate of growth were constant across states that start from different levels, the dispersion in the logarithm of the levels will stay constant but dispersion in the levels will increase.

4. Caselli and Coleman (2001) studied the U.S. structural transformation (the decline of agriculture as the dominating sector) and regional convergence (of southern to northern average wages). Their empirical findings provide a powerful explanation for the convergence pattern in the early part of the twentieth century, as illustrated in figure 2.1. Most of the regional convergence is attributable to the structural transformation: the nationwide con-

vergence of agricultural wages to nonagricultural wages and the faster rate of transition of the southern labor force from agricultural to nonagricultural jobs. Similarly, the Caselli and Coleman analysis describes the Midwest's catchup to the Northeast.

5. Barro and Sala-i-Martin (1992, 1995) in particular examine the convergence pattern in income per capita for the American states for a period that ended in the mid-1980s. As figure 2.1 illustrates, the pattern of state income convergence began to flatten about that same time.

6. The results reported in table 2.1 use the Huber-White estimator of the variance. When the traditional calculation of the variance is used in the regression model, the significance levels on all the estimated parameters are the same as those reported in table 2.1.

7. See Buchanan and Yoon 1994 for an extensive collection of readings on alternative growth models.

Chapter 3

1. See, for example, the treatment in Brealey and Myers 2000.

2. Hall and Jones (1997) provide a cogent discussion of the theoretical distinctions between explaining why some countries are rich and others are poor versus explaining why some countries grow rapidly and others grow slowly. Dawson and Stephenson (1997) find no significant relationship between volatility and growth using American state data for the period 1970–88. Their measures of state volatility generally follow the Ramey and Ramey (1995) procedures.

3. See Stata Corp. (1999, 360–69) for details of the FGLS technique. One point merits further emphasis. Income data are generally heteroskedastic, with larger variances for higher incomes than for lower incomes. As a simple illustration, from year to year Bill Gates's income may fluctuate by millions while my income may fluctuate by only thousands. This is the standard reason why income and volatility go together. The typical solution to this source of heteroskedasticity is to transform the income data into log form, as is done in the text. Beyond that, the FGLS estimation procedure estimates and then adjusts for systematic patterns in the residuals across states.

4. For a survey of the empirical literature that examines state economic performance see Crain and Lee 1999.

5. This measurement procedure also follows the technique developed by Christina Romer (1986) in a study that compared U.S. economic fluctuations in the prewar and postwar periods. Levinson (1998) provides another application of the technique, analyzing the impact of state balanced budget requirements on state economic fluctuations. As noted, the cross-country study by Ramey and Ramey (1995) uses both methods: the standard deviation in the regression model residuals and the standard deviation in innovations from the forecasted values. They conclude that the second method provides the best results in the cross-country analysis.

6. Delaware's value shown in table 3.2 is also 0.018, rounded to three digits, but slightly higher than the U.S. value.

7. The main difference between the 50-state sample and the 48-state sample lies in the magnitude of the coefficients on the Volatility indices. The estimated coefficients on all four Volatility measures are significant at the 0.05 level or higher using the 48-state sample, and three of the four coefficients are significant at the 0.01 level in the 50-state model. The magnitudes of the coefficients are consistently smaller in the 50-state sample than in the 48-state sample, which indicates that the outliers dampen the underlying relationship.

8. The positive correlation between volatility and state income levels stands in contrast to the negative relationship between volatility and income growth rates that Ramey and Ramey (1995) find using a cross-sectional sample of 97 countries.

9. To clarify, recall that estimation models used the logarithmic transformation of the income data. The results indicate that the relationship between volatility and the logarithmic transformation of income is linear. However, this means that the relationship between volatility and nonlogged income levels will be nonlinear, as the figures show.

Chapter 4

1. Wallis (2000) presents an overview and description of the major trends in American fiscal history from 1790 to 1990. For thorough, if somewhat dated, histories of American public finance, see Dewey 1934 and Studenski and Krooss 1963.

2. Throughout the remaining analysis total state taxes are defined as the sum of sales taxes (general and selective), individual income taxes, and corporation net income taxes. This definition facilitates the comparisons across states because states differ in definitions of the remaining "tax" revenue sources. For example, what some states define as a "current user charge," other states define as a "tax."

3. Subsequent chapters will address the important consequences of this structural change in state tax instruments and offer insights into the forces underlying this change.

4. To reiterate, the coefficient of variation is the standard deviation of a variable divided by its mean value. An advantage of using this measure of dispersion (as opposed to, say, the standard deviation) is that it normalizes the values for differences in the means. This makes the coefficient of variation measures of dispersion comparable between different data series (in this case between the different types of taxes), as well as over time.

5. Equation (4.2) shows the computation of the average tax rate values, and the values for each state are reported in table 4.2 for the 1969–98 period.

6. The presentation adopts the convenient notation and clear exposition of the Koester-Kormendi procedure provided by Besci (1996). The Besci

study builds upon and extends the application of the Koester-Kormendi procedure to states by Mullen and Williams (1994).

7. The analysis assumes that a state's total personal income reflects the relevant tax base. For the individual income tax this assumption is straightforward. For sales taxes, it requires consumer spending or retail sales (the direct tax base for the sales tax) to be proportional to income, which appears reasonable. As noted in the text, all prior studies estimate the MTR using total state and local taxes (including property taxes). These widely inclusive measures of tax revenues have the disadvantage of being less directly tied to personal income as the appropriate tax base. The Mullen and Williams 1994 study uses Gross State Product to proxy the aggregate tax base, but this may also be inappropriate given the inclusion of property taxes that are linked to wealth measures. State Income and Gross State Product are correlated with state wealth, and the strength of this correlation determines the precision of the parameter estimates in those studies.

8. Taxes that do not affect behavior are nondistortionary. While lump sum taxes are not collected in practice they are implicit in tax schedules that are either progressive or regressive. If the lump sum tax is positive, the tax function is said to be regressive. If the lump sum tax is negative, the tax schedule is progressive. Only if the lump sum tax is zero is the tax schedule proportional.

9. The seven states without individual income taxes are excluded from the income tax regressions: Alaska, Florida, Nevada, South Dakota, Texas, Washington, and Wyoming. In addition, I exclude from the income tax regressions the three states without an individual income tax on earned income (i.e., salaries and wages): Connecticut, New Hampshire, and Tennessee. To clarify, these three states levy individual income taxes on unearned income such as interest and dividends. I drop from the sales tax regressions the four states that do not have a general sales tax: Delaware, Montana, New Hampshire, and Oregon. These states levy some selective sales taxes, but the small revenues associated with these taxes are not of a comparable magnitude to the revenues in states with a general sales taxes.

10. In each case the modified sample period ends in 1998. The beginning years of the sample period for each of these six states are as follows: Illinois (1971), Maine (1970), Ohio (1973), Pennsylvania (1971), Rhode Island (1972), and West Virginia (1972). I also conducted the analysis using the full 1969–98 period for these states. In those regressions, the specific parameter estimates for the MTR differed from those in the modified sample periods, but none of the major conclusions was affected.

11. Numerous studies use this procedure. A few examples (listed chronologically) are Genetski and Chin 1978; Romans and Subrahmanyam 1979; Dye 1980; Plaut and Pluta 1983; Helms 1985; Wasylenko and McGuire 1985; Benson and Johnson 1986; Canto and Webb 1987; Koester and Kormendi 1989; Wei, Wallace, and Nardinelli 1991; Mullen and Williams 1994; and Besci 1996.

In fact, most analyses of state taxes prior to Mullen and Williams 1994 and Besci 1996 relied exclusively on average tax rates. Phillips and Goss 1995 provides a useful survey of state tax studies. I discuss in chapter 5 some important drawbacks in analyses based on average tax rates instead of marginal tax rates.

12.   Besci (1996) illustrates how average tax rates and marginal tax rates are related by dividing both sides of equation (4.1) by income:

$$\text{ATR}_t = (\lambda \div \text{Income}_t) + \text{MTR}. \tag{4.2a}$$

Equation (4.2a) shows that for a regressive (progressive) flat tax the average tax rate is greater (smaller) than the marginal tax rate and that the average tax rate falls (rises) when income rises. A tax is proportional when the average tax rate is the same for all levels of income. Stated differently, a flat tax schedule is progressive if ATR/MTR < 1 and regressive if ATR/MTR > 1.

Chapter 5

1.   Some studies find no effect at all, and perhaps surprisingly others suggest a positive correlation between taxes and state economic performance. For examples, see Genetski and Chin 1978; Romans and Subrahmanyam 1979; Dye 1980; Plaut and Pluta 1983; Helms 1985; Wasylenko and McGuire 1985; Benson and Johnson 1986; Canto and Webb 1987; Koester and Kormendi 1989; Wei, Wallace, and Nardinelli 1991; Mullen and Williams 1994; and Besci 1996. Phillips and Goss 1995 and Crain and Lee 1999 provide surveys of the state tax studies.

2.   Changes in the tax rate on the last taxable dollar, the "marginal tax rate," create incentives to change behavior. The average tax rate does not create behavioral changes but rather tends to reflect the changes of the marginal tax rate and changes of the tax base induced by behavior changes.

3.   The pre-Besci empirical studies generally attempt to deal with this issue in two ways. Helms (1985) pioneered the approach that adds to the regression model all sources and uses of government funds. Helms uses the average tax rate based on all state and local taxes. He finds a net negative effect on growth if taxes finance welfare transfers and a net positive effect if taxes primarily finance appropriate spending. A second approach proposes a way around including all expenditure and nontax revenue items as independent control variables (Koester and Kormindi 1989 and Mullen and Williams 1994). These studies propose that controlling for average tax rates as well as marginal tax rates isolates the effects of "revenue-neutral" fiscal policies. This approach includes both the average tax rate and the marginal tax rate in the regression equation. However, Besci (1996) demonstrates that neutrality of average revenue does not imply revenue neutrality. As an alternative, he shows that a progressivity-neutral (or, equivalently, a regressivity-neutral) tax policy comes close to isolating the distortionary effects of taxation when expenditures are not included in the regression model.

4. Besci follows at least two other studies in this regard, namely, Genetski and Chin 1978 and Mullen and Williams 1994.

5. For comparison, I also estimated the same regressions (not reported) without the Besci method of using the log differences from average state values. The signs and significances of the coefficients were quite similar to those reported in tables 5.1 and 5.2 using the log differences from the average state values.

6. Recall that Kansas happens to have the median marginal sales tax rate, which simplifies the exposition. In general, the calibration of the tax rate change needs to be assessed relative to the median tax rate across states; that is, the tax rate rises 10 percent relative to the median state. The predicted income decline of $1,375 is computed by multiplying the change in the tax rate (10 percent) times the estimated coefficient on the marginal tax rate (0.31) times the state median income ($44,340 in 1999).

7. If consumer demand is perfectly inelastic or if producer supply is perfectly inelastic, prices will rise in response to a sales tax but output would not change. If consumer demand is perfectly elastic or if producer supply is perfectly elastic, prices will not change in response to a sales tax but output would decline.

8. These commodities include: bananas, bread, Big Mac, Crisco, eggs, Kleenex, milk, Monopoly (board game), shampoo, soda, spin balance, and underwear (boys briefs).

Chapter 6

1. "... [I]n taxation, a matter of so great importance, that a very considerable degree of inequality, it appears, I believe, from the experience of all nations, is not so great an evil as a very small degree of uncertainty" (Smith 1937, 778). Gold (1983) and Sobel and Holcombe (1996) provide some historical background on the role of reliability in the analysis of taxation.

2. The asymmetric political consequences of a revenue shortfall versus a revenue windfall create a perverse incentive to be "conservative" when making state revenue projections. That is, the political fallout from cutting programs or raising taxes to cope with end-of-year deficits is large relative to the political consequences from not having implemented a tax reduction. One rarely sees end-of-year state budget surpluses being refunded to taxpayers.

3. Chapters 8 and 9 examine in further detail the effects of various constitutional rules and statutory institutional arrangements on state fiscal policies.

4. As discussed in chapter 3 (see note 5), this technique follows the procedure developed in Christina Romer (1986) and Levinson (1998).

5. The general trend over the 1968–98 period, as indicated by the median state values, has been an increase in the income tax revenues as a share of state income and a slight decline in sales tax revenues as a share of state income. As shown in chapter 4, the result of these trends has been a

displacement of sales tax revenues by income tax revenues in the composition of total state taxes. By examining the deviations from the trend, the
volatility measures are normalized around a zero mean value.

6. I note two additional details about the estimation of equation (6.1).
First, the estimation procedure uses a first-order autoregressive model to
correct for serial correlation in the error terms. Second, as noted in chapter
4, six states experienced major changes in tax structure in the early 1970s. For
these six states equation (6.1) is estimated using a slightly modified sample
period, all of which end in 1998. For beginning sample dates for these six
states see chapter 4.

7. Technically, let ϕ stand for the percent of combined taxes raised by a
tax instrument. Let σ stand for the standard deviation in the tax instrument
under a state's existing mix of sales and income taxes. The projected standard deviation assuming that the single tax instrument generated all revenues is $((1 \div \phi) \times \sigma)$. For example, suppose combined revenues equal $4
billion, ϕ for the sales tax is 25 percent, and σ for the sales tax is 0.01. The
projected standard deviation is 0.04, that is, $((1 \div 0.25) \times 0.01)$. If ϕ for the
income tax is 75 percent, and σ for the income tax is also 0.01, the projected
standard deviation is 0.013, that is, $((1 \div 0.75) \times 0.01)$.

8. For the within-state comparison I omit states that do not levy general
sales taxes or individual income taxes on earned income. See chapter 4 for a
complete discussion of the specific tax structures in each state.

9. This repeats the procedure employed in table 6.1 to make the appropriate revenue-equivalent comparisons.

Chapter 7

1. The analysis of state spending throughout the chapter omits three
states that experienced atypical spending patterns during these three decades: Alaska, Hawaii, and Wyoming. This follows the conventional practice in
the literature because the fiscal experiences of these states represent clear
statistical outliers. Data values with large deviations from the average sample
values usually exert undue influence in statistical analysis and thereby result
in biased parameter estimates. The source of the large deviations in Alaska
and Wyoming stems from their unusually heavy reliance on energy severance
taxes. In Hawaii the state government funds all public education expenditures. Other states delegate to local governments the main responsibility for
funding education for grades K–12.

2. This indicator of government growth differs slightly from that shown
in figure 7.1 simply because the states with the median income and median
spending are not the same as the state with the median ratio of spending as
a share of income. However, both measures depict a quite similar pattern in
the growth of state spending.

3. To some extent these divergent spending patterns reflect an increase
in intergovernmental transfers from the federal government to the state governments.

4. For the reasons described previously, Alaska, Hawaii, and Wyoming are omitted from the analysis, which means that 47 is the maximum possible rank. Here, the four-year averages are used to dampen the importance of a random downturn or upturn in spending that may have occurred in a single year. Comparisons based on rankings for spending in 1969 and 1998 produce similar results.

Chapter 8

1. See Poterba 1996 and 1997 for surveys of the American state litera-ture. In addition to the state studies, some researchers have analyzed how differences in the rules for developing, enacting, and enforcing budgets af-fect fiscal performance across nations. See the survey in Alesina and Perotti 1996 and the collected volume edited by Poterba and Von Hagen (1999).

2. Krause 2001 provides a survey of the scant literature on this issue. He further models a closely related issue: How do administrative agencies con-struct budget requests under conditions of uncertainty? The purpose of the Krause model is to determine the extent to which an administrative agency is willing to extract additional budgetary resources (organizational slack) in response to the uncertainty that they are experiencing. Krause contends that administrative agencies treat budgetary resources as a hedge against the un-certainty that they experience from an organizational perspective. Adminis-trative agencies view budget requests as an instrument to help buffer the or-ganization against uncertainty, thus serving as a viable means to acquire organizational slack. Krause concludes that budgetary risk-averse agencies place a premium on organizational maintenance in their attempts to obtain additional funding, and therefore respond with larger budget requests under uncertainty compared to budgetary risk-seeking or risk-neutral agencies.

3. If the agency selects the α-process and Q_H materializes, costs exceed the minimum by \$200 million (= \$900 − \$700). If it selects the β-process and Q_L materializes, costs exceed the minimum again by \$200 million (= \$500 − \$300).

4. Garrett (1999) provides a historical summary and current legal stand-ing of the presidential item veto in the United States.

5. It is interesting to note that the long-term trend in state governments has been away from biennial budgets. In 1940 only four states had annual budgets; in 1962 thirty-two states had annual budgets.

6. This hypothesis follows the theory developed in Landes and Posner 1975. See also Crain 2001 for a survey of the studies that explore the role of institutions as mechanisms that determine the durability of political transactions.

7. For examples of prior studies, see Crain and Crain 1999, Bohn and Inman 1996, Gilligan and Matsusaka 1995, Poterba 1994, and Alt and Lowry 1994. Other base-model specifications were examined that included the fol-lowing in the vector of control variables: the growth rate in income per capita, the change in the unemployment rate, and the population growth

rate. Adding these additional variables changed none of the results on the impact of volatility or the institutional variables.

8. The first-stage estimation of Expenditure Volatility uses two variables as instruments, Tax Volatility and Lame Duck. These variables are described in equation (8.4) in the text, and table 8.6 shows the results of the model that specifies Expenditure Volatility as the dependent variable.

9. The estimates based on the two-stage models appear more appropriate than those based on the single-stage models because the first-stage results indicate that Expenditure Volatility is correlated with the institutional variables. Note that in the Instrumental Variables model the coefficient on Expenditure Volatility, 5.87, is more than twice the size of this coefficient in the single-stage model, 2.51. In other words, the endogeneity problem results in a substantial downward bias in this parameter estimate.

10. Recall that total tax revenues include sales taxes, individual income taxes, and corporation net income taxes.

11. For example, if a state had no gubernatorial term limit, the Lame Duck variable equals 0. If a state has a one-term limit the variable equals 1. If a state's governors faced a term limit in 14 of the 29 years, the Lame Duck variable equals 0.5. This variable follows from the study by Besley and Case (1995b).

Chapter 9

1. These four categories generally follow the divisions adopted by the U.S. Census Bureau. I combine spending for public welfare, health, and hospitals into a single category and do the same for police protection and corrections. The Census Bureau reports separately the spending levels for these programs.

2. The coefficient of variation is the standard deviation divided by the mean. The analysis here excludes Alaska, Hawaii, and Wyoming.

3. The two ideology variables are obtained from Berry, Ringquist, Fording, and Hanson 1998. The ideology measures described in this 1998 article were updated through 1996 for the government index and through 1997 for the citizen index at the time of this writing. The construction of these indices relies on roll call voting scores of state congressional delegations (ADA and COPE scores), the outcomes of congressional elections, the partisan division of state legislatures, the party of the governor, and various assumptions regarding voters and state political elites. A full description of the methodologies employed and the data set are available at <http://pubadm/fsu.edu/archives>. The website also provides references to the growing body of papers (mostly by political scientists) that have used these and other political ideology indices.

4. As in chapter 8, the models are estimated using panel data that begin in 1970. The models containing the Citizen Ideology index end in 1997, and the models that contain the Government Ideology index end in 1996. The dependent variables in all models denominate spending in terms of real (2000)

dollars per capita. Table 9.A1 in the appendix to this chapter provides summary statistics for all variables used in the analysis.

5. I investigated the potential endogeneity problem in this specification, namely, that political ideology might jointly determine fiscal institutions and spending and thereby bias the single-stage parameter estimates. Using a pooled probit regression model, I find a significant relationship between ideology and the adoption of balanced budget rules and supermajority requirements. However, the results reported in the text were not materially different from those obtained from a more complex two-stage specification that attempts to endogenize these two fiscal rules.

6. The Citizen and Government Ideology indices are significantly correlated, both within a state over time and across states. A FGLS regression of Government Ideology against Citizen Ideology yields a coefficient of 1.2, with a t-statistic of 22 and an overall R-squared of 0.47. For this reason, each index is examined separately rather than combined into a single regression model.

References

Abrams, Burton, and William Dougan. 1986. "The Effects of Constitutional Restraints on Government Spending." *Public Choice* 49:101–16.

Advisory Commission on Intergovernmental Relations. 1987. *Fiscal Discipline in the Federal System: National Reform and the Experience of the States.* Washington, DC: A-107.

Aizenman, Joshua, and Nancy Marion. 1993. "Policy Uncertainty, Persistence and Growth." *Review of International Economics* 1 (2): 145–63.

Alesina, Alberto, and Roberto Perotti. 1996. "Fiscal Discipline and the Budget Process." *American Economic Review* 86 (2): 401–7.

Alt, J. E., and R. C. Lowry. 1994. "Divided Government, Fiscal Institutions, and Budget Deficits: Evidence from the States." *American Political Science Review* 88:811–28.

Barone, Michael, and Grant Ujifusa. Biennial Editions, 1968 through 2000. *The Almanac of American Politics.* Washington, DC: National Journal Group.

Barro, Robert J. 1979. "On the Determination of the Public Debt." *Journal of Political Economy* 87 (5, October): 940–71.

———. 1991. "Economic Growth in a Cross Section of Countries." *Quarterly Journal of Economics* 106:407–44.

———. 1997. *Determinants of Economic Growth: A Cross-Country Empirical Study.* Cambridge, MA: MIT Press.

Barro, Robert J., and X. Sala-i-Martin. 1992. "Convergence." *Journal of Political Economy* 100:223–51.

———. 1995. *Economic Growth.* Cambridge, MA: MIT Press.

Benson, Bruce L., and Ronald N. Johnson. 1986. "The Lagged Impact of State and Local Taxes on Economic Activity and Political Behavior." *Economic Inquiry* 24 (3): 389–402.

Bernanke, Ben S. 1983. "Irreversibility, Uncertainty, and Cyclical Investment." *Quarterly Journal of Economics* 98 (1, February): 85–106.

Berry, William D., et al. 1998. "Measuring Citizen and Government Ideology in the American States, 1960–93." *American Journal of Political Science* 42 (1, January): 327–48.

Besci, Zsolt. 1996. "Do State and Local Taxes Affect Relative State Growth?" *Economic Review* 81 (2): 18–36.

Besley, Timothy, and Anne Case. 1995a. " Incumbent Behavior: Vote-Seeking,

Tax-Setting, and Yardstick Competition." *American Economic Review* 85 (1): 25–45.

———. 1995b. "Does Electoral Accountability Affect Economic Policy Choices?" *Quarterly Journal of Economics* 110 (3, August): 769–98.

Besley, Timothy, and Harvey S. Rosen. 1999. "Sales Taxes and Prices: An Empirical Analysis." *National Tax Journal* 52 (2): 157–78.

Black, Fischer. 1987. *Business Cycles and Equilibrium.* Cambridge, MA: Blackwell.

Bohn, Henning, and Robert P. Inman. 1996. "Balanced Budget Rules and Public Deficits: Evidence from the U.S. States." *Carnegie-Rochester Conference Series on Public Policy* 45:13–76.

Bradbury, John Charles, and W. Mark Crain. 2002. "Bicameral Legislatures and Political Compromise." *Southern Economic Journal* 68 (3): 646–59.

Brealey, Richard A., and Stewart C. Myers. 2000. *Principles of Corporate Finance.* Boston: Irwin/McGraw-Hill.

Buchanan, James M., and Y. Yoon. 1994. *The Return to Increasing Returns.* Ann Arbor: University of Michigan Press.

Canjels, Eugene, and Mark W. Watson. 1997. "Estimating Deterministic Trends in the Presence of Serially Correlated Error Terms." *Review of Economics and Statistics* 79 (2): 184–200.

Canto, V., and R. I. Webb. 1987. "The Effect of State Fiscal Policy on State Relative Economic Performance." *Southern Economic Journal* 54 (July): 186–202.

Carter, John, and David Schap. 1990. "Line-Item Veto: Where Is Thy Sting?" *Journal of Economic Perspectives* 4:103–18.

Caselli, Francesco, and Wilbur John Coleman II. 2001. "The U.S. Structural Transformation and Regional Convergence: A Reinterpretation." *Journal of Political Economy* 109 (3): 584–616.

Clingermayer, James, and B. Dan Wood. 1995. "Disentangling Patterns of State Debt Financing. *American Journal of Political Science* 89 (1): 108–20.

Council of State Governments. Biennial Editions, 1968 through 2000. *The Book of the States.* Lexington, KY.

Crain, W. Mark. 1999. "Districts, Diversity and Fiscal Biases: Evidence from the American States." *Journal of Law and Economics* 23 (2): 675–98.

———. 2001. "Institutions, Durability, and the Value of Political Transactions." In *The Elgar Companion to Public Choice,* ed. William F. Shughart II and Laura Razzolini, 183–96. Cheltenham, UK: Edward Elgar.

Crain, W. Mark, and Nicole V. Crain. 1998. "Fiscal Consequences of Budget Baselines." *Journal of Public Economics* 67 (3): 421–36.

Crain, W. Mark, and Katherine J. Lee. 1999. "Economic Growth Regressions for the American States: A Sensitivity Analysis." *Economic Inquiry* 37 (2): 242–57.

Crain, W. Mark, and James C. Miller III. 1990. "Budget Process and Spending Growth." *William and Mary Law Review* 31 (4): 1021–46.

Crain, W. Mark, and Timothy J. Muris. 1995. "Legislative Organization of Fiscal Policy." *Journal of Law and Economics* 38 (2): 311–33.

Crain, W. Mark, and L. K. Oakley. 1995. "The Politics of Infrastructure." *Journal of Law and Economics* 38 (1): 1–17.

Crain, W. Mark, and R. D. Tollison. 1993. "Time Inconsistency and Fiscal Policy: Empirical Analysis of U.S. States, 1969–89." *Journal of Public Economics* 51 (2): 153–59.

Crihfield, John B., and Martin P. H. Panggabean. 1995. "Growth and Convergence in U.S. Cities." *Journal of Urban Economics* 38:138–65.

Dawson, John W., and E. Frank Stephenson. 1997. "The Link Between Volatility and Growth: Evidence from the States." *Economic Letters* 55: 365–69.

Dewey, Davis R. 1934. *Financial History of the United States.* New York: Augustus Kelley.

Duncan, Philip D., and Christine C. Lawrence. Biennial Editions, 1968 through 2000. *Politics in America.* Washington, DC: CQ Press.

Dye, T. R. 1980. "Taxing, Spending, and Economic Growth in the American States." *Journal of Politics* 42 (4, November): 1085–107.

Easterly, William, and Sergio Rebelo. 1993. "Fiscal Policy and Economic Growth." *Journal of Monetary Economics* 32:417–58.

Eichengreen, Barry J. 1992. "Should the Maastrict Treaty Be Saved?" International Finance Section working paper no. 74, Princeton University, Princeton, NJ.

Elder, Harold E. 1992. "Exploring the Tax Revolt: An Analysis of the Effectiveness of State Tax and Expenditure Limitation Laws." *Public Finance Quarterly* 20 (1): 47–63.

Garand, James, and Rebecca Hendrick. 1991. "Expenditure Tradeoffs in the American States: A Longitudinal Test, 1948–1984." *Western Political Quarterly* 44:915–40.

Garrett, Elizabeth. 1999. "Accountability and Restraint: The Federal Budget Process and the Line Item Veto Act." *Cardozo Law Review* 20 (3): 871–937.

Genetski, R. J., and Y. D. Chin. 1978. "The Impact of State and Local Taxes on Economic Growth." Chicago: Harris Economic Research Office Service, November 3.

Gilligan, Thomas W., and Keith Krehbiel. 1989. "Collective Choice without Procedural Commitment." In *Models of Strategic Choice,* ed. Peter C. Ordeshook. Ann Arbor: University of Michigan Press.

Gilligan, Thomas W., and John G. Matsusaka. 1995. "Deviations from Constituent Interests: The Role of Legislative Structure and Political Parties in the States." *Economic Inquiry* 33:383–401.

———. 2001. "Fiscal Policy, Legislative Size, and Political Parties: Evidence from State and Local Governments in the First Half of the Twentieth Century." *National Tax Journal* 54 (1): 57–82.

Gold, Steven D. 1983. "Preparing for the Next Recession: Rainy Day Funds and Other Tools for the States." Legislative Finance paper no. 41, National Conference of State Legislatures, Denver.

————. 1992. "State Government Experience with Balanced Budget Requirements: Relevance to Federal Proposals." In *The Balanced Budget Amendment,* U.S. House of Representatives, Committee on the Budget, 202–10. Washington, DC: U.S. Government Printing Office.

Gramlich, Edward M. 1991. "The 1991 State and Local Fiscal Crises." *Brookings Papers on Economic Activity* 2:249–87.

Grier, Kevin, and Gordon Tullock. 1989. "An Empirical Analysis of Cross-National Economic Growth, 1951–80." *Journal of Monetary Economics* 24 (2, September): 259–76.

Groves, Harold, and C. Harry Kahn. 1952. "The Stability of State and Local Tax Yields." *American Economic Review,* 42 (1): 87–102.

Hall, Robert E., and Charles I. Jones. 1997. "Levels of Economic Activity across Countries." *American Economic Review* 87 (2): 173–77.

Helms, L. Jay. 1985. "The Effect of State and Local Taxes on Economic Growth: A Time Series—Cross Section Approach." *Review of Economics and Statistics* 67, no. 4 (November): 574–82.

Hines, James R., Jr. 1996. "Altered States: Taxes and the Location of Foreign Direct Investment in America." *American Economic Review* 86 (5): 1076–94.

Holmes, Thomas J. 1998. "The Effect of State Policies on the Location of Manufacturing: Evidence from State Borders." *Journal of Political Economy* 106 (4): 667–705.

Holtz-Eakin, Douglas. 1988. "The Line Item Veto and Public Sector Budgets: Evidence from the States." *Journal of Public Economics* 36:269–92.

Inman, Robert. 1997. "Do Balanced Budget Rules Work? U.S. Experience and Possible Lessons for the EMU." Institut fur Weltwirtschaft a der Universitat Kiel Symposia and Conference Proceedings. Tubingen: Mohr (Siebeck): 307–32.

Inman, Robert, and Henning Bohn. 1996. "Balanced-Budget Rules and Public Deficits: Evidence from the U.S. States." *Carnegie-Rochester Conference Series on Public Policy* 45:13–76.

Ireland, Peter N. 1994. "Two Perspectives of Growth and Taxes." *Economic Quarterly* 80 (1): 1–17.

Kearns, Paula S. 1994. "State Budget Periodicity: An Analysis of the Determinants and the Effect on State Spending." *Journal of Policy Analysis and Management* 13 (2): 331–62.

Knight, Brian G. 2000. "Supermajority Voting Requirements for Tax Increases: Evidence from the States." *Journal of Public Economics* 76 (1): 41–67.

Knight, Brian G., and Arik Levinson. 1999. "Rainy Day Funds and State Government Savings." *National Tax Journal* 52 (3): 459–72.

Koester, Reinhard B., and Roger Kormendi. 1989. "Taxation, Aggregate Activity and Economic Growth: Cross-Country Evidence on Some Supply-Side Hypotheses." *Economic Inquiry* 27 (3): 367–86.

Kormendi, Roger, and Phillip McGuire. 1985. "Macroeconomic Determinants of Growth." *Journal of Monetary Economics* 16 (2, September): 141–63.

Krause, George A. 2001. "Budget Requests and Agency Decision Making under Uncertainty." Mimeo, University of South Carolina, Columbia.

Krugman, Paul. 1991. *Geography and Trade.* Cambridge, MA: MIT Press.

Kydland, Finn E., and Edward C. Prescott. 1980. "A Competitive Theory of Fluctuations and the Feasibility and Desirability of Stabilization Policy." In *Rational Expectations and Economic Policy,* ed. Stanley Fisher. Chicago: University of Chicago Press.

Landes, William M., and Richard A. Posner. 1975. "The Independent Judiciary in an Interest Group Perspective." *Journal of Law and Economics* 18:875–901.

Levinson, Arik. 1998. "Balanced Budgets and Business Cycles: Evidence from the States." *National Tax Journal* 51 (4): 715–32.

Lowry, Robert C., James E. Alt, and Karen E. Ferree. 1998. "Fiscal Policy Outcomes and Electoral Accountability in American States." *American Political Science Review* 92 (4): 759–74.

Lucas, Robert E., and Nancy L. Stokey. 1983. "Optimal Fiscal and Monetary Policy in a World without Capital." *Journal of Monetary Economics* 12 (1, January): 55–94.

Mankiw, G., D. Romer, and D. Weil. 1992. "A Contribution to the Empirics of Economic Growth." *Quarterly Journal of Economics* 107:407–37.

Matsusaka, John G. 1992. "Economics of Direct Legislation." *Quarterly Journal of Economics* 107 (2): 541–71.

———. 1995. "Fiscal Effects of the Voter Initiative: Evidence from the Last Thirty Years." *Journal of Political Economy* 103 (31): 587–623.

Milesi-Ferretti, Gian Maria, and Nouriel Rouibini. 1998. "Growth Effects of Income and Consumption Taxes." *Journal of Money, Credit, and Banking* 30 (4): 721–44.

Mirman, Leonard. 1971. "Uncertainty and Optimal Consumption Decisions." *Econometrica* 39 (1): 179–85.

Mullen, J. K., and M. Williams. 1994. "Marginal Tax Rates and State Economic Growth." *Regional Science and Urban Economics* 24:687–705.

Phillips, J. M., and E. P. Goss. 1995. "The Effect of State and Local Taxes on Economic Development." *Southern Economic Journal* 62 (2): 320–33.

Pindyck, Robert S. 1991. "Irreversibility, Uncertainty, and Investment." *Journal of Economic Literature* 29 (3, September): 1110–48.

Plaut, T. R., and J. E. Pluta. 1983. "Business Climate, Taxes, and Expenditures and State Industrial Growth in the United States." *Southern Economic Journal* 50:99–119.

Poterba, James M. 1994. "State Responses to Fiscal Crises: The Effects of Budgetary Institutions and Politics." *Journal of Political Economy* 102: 799–821.

———. 1995. "Capital Budgets, Borrowing Rules, and State Capital Spending." *Journal of Public Economics* 56:165–87.

———. 1996. "Budget Institutions and Fiscal Policy in the U.S. States." *American Economic Review* 86 (2): 395–400.

———. 1997. "Do Budget Rules Work?" In *Fiscal Policy: Lessons from Economic Research,* ed. Alan J. Auerbach, 53–86. Cambridge, MA: MIT Press.

Poterba, James M., and Juergen Von Hagen, eds. 1999. *Fiscal Institutions and Fiscal Performance.* Chicago: University of Chicago Press.

Pritchett, Lant. 1997. "Divergence, Big Time." *Journal of Economic Perspectives* 11:3–17.

Ramey, Garey, and Valerie A. Ramey. 1991. "Technology Commitment and the Cost of Economic Fluctuations." Cambridge, MA: NBER working paper no. 3755.

———. 1995. "Cross-Country Evidence on the Link between Volatility and Growth." *American Economic Review* 85 (5, December): 1138–52.

Riker, William. 1980. "Implications for the Disequilibrium of Majority Rule for the Study of Institutions." *American Political Science Review* 74:432–46.

Romans, T., and G. Subrahmanyam. 1979. "State and Local Taxes, Transfers and Regional Economic Growth." *Southern Economic Journal* 46:435–44.

Romer, Christina D. 1986. "Is the Stabilization of the Postwar Economy a Figment of the Data?" *American Economic Review* 76 (3): 314–34.

Romer, Paul. 1986. "Increasing Returns and Long-Run Growth." *Journal of Political Economy* 94 (5): 1002–37.

Rueben, Kim. 1995. "Tax Limitation and Government Growth: The Effect of State Tax and Expenditure Limits on State and Local Government." Mimeo, Department of Economics, MIT, Cambridge, MA.

Shadbegian, Ronald J. 1996. "Do Tax and Expenditure Limitations Affect the Size and Growth of State Government?" *Contemporary Economic Policy* 14:22–35.

Smith, Adam. [1776] 1937. *The Wealth of Nations.* Reprint, New York: Modern Library.

Sobel, Russell S., and Randall G. Holcombe. 1996. "The Impact of State Rainy Day Funds in Easing State Fiscal Crises during the 1990–1991 Recession." *Public Budgeting and Finance* 16 (3): 28–48.

Stata Corp. 1999. *Stata Statistical Software: Release 6.0.* College Station, TX: Stata Corporation.

Stokey, N. L., and S. Rebelo. 1995. "Growth Effects of Flat-Rate Taxes." *Journal of Political Economy* 103 (3): 519–50.

Studenski, Paul, and Herman E. Krooss. 1963. *Financial History of the United States.* New York: McGraw-Hill.

Tweedie, Jack. 1994. "Resources Rather Than Needs: A State-Centered Model of Welfare Policymaking." *American Journal of Political Science* 38 (3): 651–72.

U.S. General Accounting Office. 1987. *Budget Issues, Current Status and Recent Trends of State Biennial and Annual Budgeting.* Washington, DC: General Accounting Office.

————. 1993. *Balanced Budget Requirements: State Experiences and Implications for the Federal Government.* GAO/AFMD-93-58BR. Washington, DC: General Accounting Office.

Wallis, John Joseph. 2000. "American Government Finance in the Long Run." *Journal of Economic Perspectives* 14 (1): 61–82.

Wasylenko, M. J., and T. McGuire. 1985. "Jobs and Taxes: The Effect of Business Climate on States' Employment Growth Rates." *National Tax Journal* 38:497–511.

Webber, Carolyn, and Aaron Wildavsky. 1980. *A History of Taxation and Expenditure in the Western World.* New York: Simon and Schuster.

Wei Yu, Myles S. Wallace, and Clark Nardinelli. 1991. "State Growth Rates: Taxes, Spending and Catching Up." *Public Finance Quarterly* 19 (1): 80–93.

Zarnowitz, Victor, and Louis Lambros. 1987. "Consensus and Uncertainty in Economic Prediction." *Journal of Political Economy* 95 (3): 591–621.

Zarnowitz, Victor, and Geoffrey Moore. 1986. "Major Changes in Cycle Behavior." In *The American Business Cycle: Continuity and Change,* ed. Robert Gordon, 519–72. Chicago: University of Chicago Press:

Index